The Saddle

IN THEORY AND PRACTICE

The Saddle

IN THEORY AND PRACTICE

Elwyn Hartley Edwards

J A ALLEN
London

British Library Cataloguing in Publication Data
Hartley, Edwards, Elwyn 1927–
    The Saddle
    1. Livestock: Horses, Saddlery
    I. Title
    636.10837

ISBN 0–85131–526–7

Published in Great Britain in 1990 by
J. A. Allen & Company Limited
1 Lower Grosvenor Place
London SW1W 0EL

Photoset by Waveney Typesetters, Norwich
Book production Bill Ireson
Printed in Great Britain by
St Edmundsbury Press Limited, Bury St Edmunds, Suffolk

Contents

List of Illustrations

To the saddlery trade of Walsall (warts and all), recognising its position as the world's centre for the manufacture of horse equipment for some two hundred years.

1: Historical Development

The first saddle built on a wooden framework or 'tree' seems to have been the invention of the Sarmatians, originally a nomadic horse-people living on the Volga steppe lands of the Ukraine. By the second century BC they had overthrown their formidable neighbours, the Scythian horse-archers, and had spread into the lands bordering the Black Sea.

Largely because of the excavation of the frozen Pazyryk tombs in Siberia, much has been learnt about the customs and life-style of the Scythians, who otherwise left no record of their long domination of the Asian steppes.

The first excavations took place in 1929 and were continued after the Second World War. The contents of the tombs had been encased in a bed of ice from about the year 432 BC and as a result the equipment and even the very horses, which, in accordance with the customs of central Asia, had been interred along with the departed chieftains, were preserved virtually intact together with their deceased owners.

The Scythian saddle, as might be expected of a people steeped in an all-pervading horse-culture, was an essentially practical piece of equipment. Moreover, its construction, even at that early date in the man-horse relationship, reveals what one must suppose to be an instinctive recognition of the fundamental principles involved in the fitting of a saddle. One can hardly envisage these fierce horsemen, much given to decorating their saddle bows with the heads of their vanquished enemies, sitting down to consider the niceties of saddle design, but they did, none the less, produce saddles far in advance of those used by the civilised races of antiquity, Greece and Rome. Among the horse-peoples of the world, the Scythian saddle persisted, in its essentials, for many centuries.

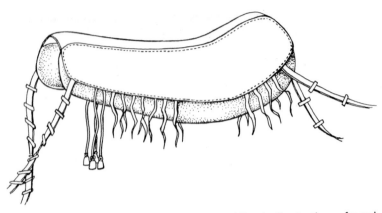

An artist's sketch of an early Scythian saddle similar to those found in the frozen tombs of Pazyryk

It was made of felt and leather and comprised two leather pads, or oblong cushions, stuffed with deer hair. The pads lay on either side of the spine, ensuring that the rider's weight was carried over the dorsal muscles and ribs. The spine itself was consequently quite free from any sort of pressure that would cause galling and/or inhibit the natural movement. The pads were joined together by wood arches at front and rear, or sometimes by a connecting piece of felt or leather laid from end to end.

Under the saddle a felt cloth or 'numnah' was placed; those discovered at Pazyryk are extravagantly embellished with all sorts of fine appliqué work. The whole was kept in place by a girth and breast-band, and often by a sort of breeching that passed round the quarters. The saddle of the Argentine gaucho, allowing for the addition of stirrups, is not much dissimilar, and when the American Indian took to riding he made a saddle that was almost an exact replica of that used by the Scythians around two thousand years previously. (In fact, the similarity is not quite as surprising as it may seem, for it is not impossible to conjecture that while the land bridges still existed between the American continent and the Old World, Asian nomads could have crossed over them to settle in North America and form that country's indigenous population. And the saddle? An atavistic memory, perhaps, along with the retention of practices common to both peoples that are too numerous to be entirely coincidental.)

The Sarmatians broke with the steppe tradition, producing a saddle that is recognisable as a forerunner of the conventional designs (at least the very early ones) with which a modern rider would be familiar.

They did so for the very good reason that they, unlike the Scythians and Parthians, who were horse-archers, had developed a heavy cavalry arm that relied on the shock tactic of a concerted charge.

These barbarian warriors who, like their predecessors and even their successors to this day, considered it beneath them to walk – an exercise at which they were, indeed, most inept and unusually awkward – continued to make some use of the bow but their principal weapon was the lance.

Throwing javelins had been employed by mounted troops before the Sarmatians' time, but they were the first horsemen to use the much heavier lance in close order and they set a pattern for the world's cavalry that persisted almost up to the demise of the mounted arm. In reality, the Sarmatian 'lance' was a long, very heavy, iron-tipped pole (called by the Greeks a 'barge pole'). It was so heavy that it had to be held in both hands. When it was couched underarm in the conventional manner, it had, additionally, to be supported by a hooked bar attachment fastened to the horse's neck.

For such a weapon to be used effectively by horsemen acting in concert against bodies of infantry, it was necessary to adopt a far more upright position than that assumed by the horse-archer and, above all, it was essential that the horseman should not be dislodged at the moment of impact.

The steppe saddle was of no help in that respect, so the Sarmatians built a boat-shaped saddle on a frame of wood. It had a front and rear arch joined by wooden side-bars resting on each side of the spine. It rose to a high peak at front and rear and afforded considerable security, even though the general introduction of the stirrup was still two or three hundred years away. As he struck into the enemy ranks, the horseman obtained additional support by bracing himself against the cantle.

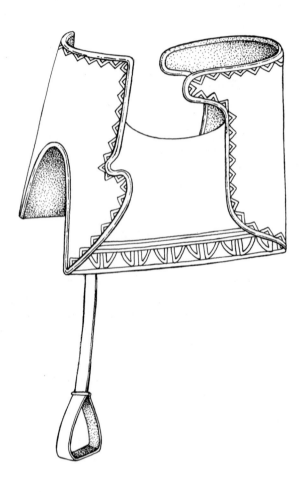

The saddle of the Middle Ages. It must have been virtually impossible to fall out of this model. Note the forward position of the stirrup bar

The Sarmatian saddle made its appearance about the beginning of the Christian era, the stirrup following perhaps two hundred years later and becoming commonly used in the area encompassed by China, central India and the Black Sea during the first four hundred years after the death of Christ. It did not, however, come into use in Europe until the eighth century A D.

From this early saddle of the steppe barbarians, that of the Middle Ages developed – the saddle of the armoured knight that was to be a principal influence in design right up to the twentieth century.

In time, both the light horsemen of the world, who were principally of Eastern origin, as well as the heavy cavalry of Europe, embraced the deeply dipped seat for reasons of security. The difference was in the positioning of the stirrup bar, or, more correctly, the attachment point of the stirrup leather.

Europe developed the heavy cavalryman, mounted, ultimately, on the heaviest, strongest horse that could be found, although the horses of the Middle Ages were not as big as is generally supposed and could certainly not have been compared with the massively built heavy horses of today. The cavalry's main tactic was a shattering charge, and its success in breaking the enemy line was dependent on the combination of weight and impetus. The position of the horseman under these circumstances was always inclined towards the rear, a posture (perhaps, indeed, an attitude of mind) that was retained in Europe long after the need for it had passed. The medieval knight, like the Sarmatians before him, braced himself between the cantle and the stirrup, with leg straight and extended to the front, the better to withstand the shock of violent contact with closely packed ranks of foot soldiers. To help him maintain this optimum position, the stirrup leathers were fastened to the *front* of the saddle, compelling him to adopt a straight, forward-thrust leg. In eighteenth-century prints depicting the movements of the High School, the riders are shown employing the same straight-leg position to conform with the stirrup bar's placement at the front of the saddle. The work of the Austrian artist, Johann Elias Ridinger, which is characterised by great

The rider in this eighteenth-century picture of Johann Elias Ridinger is shown employing the straight leg position which conformed with the position of the stirrup

accuracy of detail as well as a mastery of line and composition, illustrates this point very clearly.

What is surprising is that the position of the bar in Europe should have remained virtually unchanged for a whole millenium, right from that historic moment on the field of Poitiers in AD 732, when Charles Martel led his Christian knights against the Moors who were seeking to effect the conquest of Europe. (The engagement at Poitiers, in which the Moors were defeated, is the first recorded occasion on which a body of European cavalry employed the stirrup.) Nor was that the end of it – the stirrup bar, in all too many instances, continued to be placed too far forward for at least another two hundred years, without any more than a handful of horsemen appreciating the significance of its position in relation to the shape of the saddle and the inclination of the flap.

The light horsemen, exemplified by successive waves of horse-peoples from Asia and the East, were individually better riders than those of Europe, if less disposed to accept the restraints required for disciplined team action.

Their tactic of tip-and-run, swift-moving harassment and the lightning strike delivered to the enemy's flank or rear, was the opposite of Europe's 'steel wall of chivalry'. Their horses were light, wiry and swift and they sat them in a completely different way. They used a shortened stirrup, sat with a bent leg and inclined the trunk *forward* – a seat virtually identical to that which we are encouraged to adopt today when riding across country.

To ride like that it was necessary for the stirrup bar to be placed further back. In the high-peaked, dipped-seat saddles still employed by Eastern horsemen, that involves the bar, or point of attachment, being placed towards the middle of the saddle, almost under the rider's seat, as it were, so that the lay of the leathers 'divides' the flap into equal parts. Mongols of the thirteenth century (much shorter in the leg and more thickset than Europeans) adopted this seat and there are numerous depictions of Hungarians (themselves descendants of the steppe horsemen) and Polish horsemen, from the fifteenth century onwards, riding in a forward position with a shortened leather. None, perhaps, exemplifies the *beau idéal* of the light cavalry-

Rembrandt's picture exemplifying the *beau idéal* of the light cavalryman. This Polish horseman of centuries ago sat forward in what is to all intents a modern cross-country seat

man better than Rembrandt's vivid picture of a Polish horseman in the field armed *cap-à-pie* with sabre, thrusting sword, short bow and a quiverful of arrows, and sitting in a very modern seat.

Subsequent saddles retained many of the design features of the medieval saddle, although much scaled down.

The Renaissance

The next step in the saddle's development occurred during the Renaissance (c. 1500–1600) when the enthusiasm for school riding led to what has come to be known as 'classical' riding. If we interpret 'classical' as belonging to the authoritative arts of Greek and Roman antiquity, it was an extension and an enhancement of the techniques practised by horsemen like the Greek general, Xenophon (c. 430–356 BC). In the Roman (Byzantine) circus, too, movements like the *tripudium* (in modern parlance *piaffe*) were certainly not unknown. Byzantine practices survived in the later European circuses and there is pictorial evidence of medieval horses performing recognisable High School leaps above the ground.

It is often claimed that the immediate inspiration for the Renaissance schools was the movements practised by the medieval knight, designed to discourage and strike terror into foot soldiers bold enough to attempt to unhorse a mounted warrior. There can be no doubt that the warhorse of the Middle Ages was sometimes well enough schooled to perform relatively advanced movements but the extent of the influence exerted on subsequent generations of horsemen is less certain.

However, it cannot be disputed that it was the medieval saddle that became the saddle of the Renaissance and the *selle royale* of classical equitation, nor that it was translated into the saddle of the Western cowboy. The sixteenth-century *conquistadores* who reintroduced the horse to the American continent, where the species had been extinct for eight to ten thousand years, took with them their equipment as well as the systems of training that they had acquired during the Moorish occupation of the Iberian Peninsula. In an adapted form, the saddle of Cortes and Pizarro became that of the Californian reinsman, and the latter still schools his horses on the system of the hackamore (*jaquima, hakma* in Arabic) which has its origins long, long ago in the Middle East.

Indeed, in the development of the *selle royale* it is possible to perceive the Iberian influence, which is hardly surprising as the revival of scientific riding was founded fairly and squarely on the Spanish horse. During the seven-hundred-year occupation

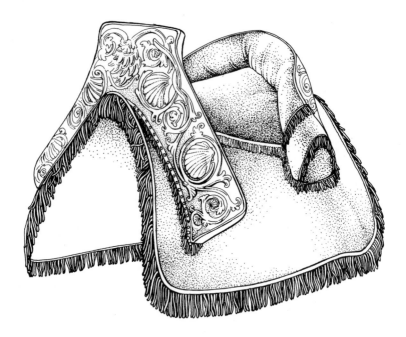

(*Above*) The *selle royale* of classical equitation. A similar saddle is used at the Spanish Riding School Vienna and it is still made in Spain and Portugal to this day. In an adapted form it has become the Western saddle of the Californian reinsman. (*Opposite*) A modern Western saddle showing clearly the influence of the European Renaissance

of the Moors, two schools of riding existed side by side in the peninsula. The Eastern, Moorish seat, with shortened stirrup, was termed '*à la gineta*' and the long straight-legged position, with the rider inclined behind the vertical plane, was called '*à la brida*'. Iberian horsemen of the Renaissance and after prided themselves on their ability to ride in both seats.

The former seat, however, depended on the stirrup attachment being placed somewhat to the rear. It is placed in that position on the Western saddle, even though the rider uses a longish leather, and by the eighteenth century this design feature was incorporated in the *selle royale*. Illustrations in

Guérinière's *Ecole de Cavalerie* (1751) show riders using a long leather, certainly, but with a bent knee. The nineteenth–century riders in Vienna's Spanish Riding School, whose school saddle derives directly from the *selle royale*, bent the knee somewhat more, while today's school riders carry the lower leg even further back. By the nineteenth century the School saddles had acquired a shaped flap with the panel following the line of the latter, in contrast to the almost square flap and panel of the sixteenth-century *selle royale.*

(Similar saddles are in general use in Spain and Portugal today and remain unquestionably a part of the equipment of the *rejoneador* who faces the fighting bulls in the arenas of Portugal.)

Minus the supporting rolls lying across the pommel and at the cantle, this became the hunting saddle of England, although during its evolutionary years it retained a vestige of its former glory in respect of the supportive padding.

Most of the early saddles, to whatever part of the world they belonged, carried the rider's weight very effectively on the dorsal muscles on either side of the spine and there was certainly no danger of either the fore-arch or the cantle galling the horse. The rider, however, sat raised well above the back, almost as though in a sort of *howdah*, and without the close contact we require today.

The movement to position the rider closer to his horse began in the sixteenth century and by the eighteenth and nineteenth centuries, when hunting had become firmly established in Britain, the saddle often allowed a degree of contact just as good as that obtainable from the saddles of today. None the less, the best of these saddles were constructed so as to spread the weight of the rider over the full extent of a relatively large bearing surface. It was a very necessary requirement in times when men spent long hours in the saddle and covered distances which would be beyond the comprehension of modern riders.

At Waterloo, in 1815, the Duke of Wellington rode his charger, Copenhagen, who stood only a shade over 15 h.h., for 39 hours between June 16–18. He covered some 97 km (60 mi) on each of the first two days and on the third, the day of the battle, he was in the saddle for 15 hours, galloping over the field to wherever his line was threatened by the French attack. On the day following the battle he rode Copenhagen to Brussels, where the horse still had enough energy to break away from his groom and gallop round the town. Copenhagen was probably carrying 86 kg (13 st 7 lb) and his rider was, by all accounts, not the most elegant of horsemen.

It is recorded that the staff of General Blücher, commanding the Prussian allies, were much impressed by Copenhagen's saddle and accoutrements, which included an ingeniously contrived 'writing desk'!

In fact, English saddlery of the period enjoyed a high

reputation throughout Europe for quality and craftsmanship; a reputation that was maintained up to the 1960s.

Saddles similar in type were, of course, made throughout Europe, but it was the English hunting saddle, in company with English clothes, that was acknowledged as being the finest available. (The Spanish Riding School, in addition to its 'school saddles', still maintains a complement of 'English saddles' that are used extensively in the training and day-to-day riding of its Lippizaners. They are by no means the best examples of the English product and they are, for the most part, very elderly, typifying the type of saddles produced at the turn of the century. The expertise of the riders compensates for the failings of the saddles in terms of both design and construction; but then, horsemen of that calibre, riding five to six hours each day, should, one imagines, be capable of sitting effectively on a piece of barbed wire.)

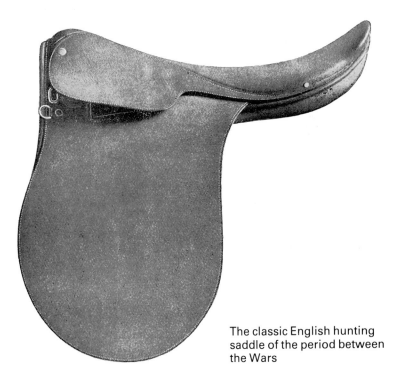

The classic English hunting saddle of the period between the Wars

English coats, breeches and boots were all distinguished by the excellence of cut and material, and the same qualities characterised English saddlery. At its very best it represented a masterpiece of understatement and well-bred restraint, while combining the best available materials with a typical workman-like appearance. The unique sporting art of the eighteenth and nineteenth centuries is full of telling examples to support what might otherwise be regarded as a somewhat chauvinistic assertion.

Although, in general, the construction of the best saddles did allow the horseman to feel close to his horse, despite the bulk caused by the panel being continued to the full length of the flap, the bearing surface on the back was sufficiently great to distribute the weight over a significantly large area. It is the effective distribution of weight that makes the Western saddle pre-eminent in the field of distance riding, when long hours are spent in the saddle. The saddle itself, together with its thick saddle blanket, is heavy in comparison with an English-type saddle but the bearing surface is commensurately large.

So where, in the modern context, did this paragon among saddles fail? The answer is that within the context of its time it was not a failure at all. After all, generations of hard-riding foxhunters, even without the benefit of present-day equestrian theory, managed very well in these saddles and performed feats quite beyond the capacity of 90 per cent of today's riders. Would Wellington and Copenhagen have done any better in a modern saddle? I think not.

Where the hunting saddle failed was in respect of the *modern* requirement, which asks for greater precision and more demanding and advanced standards in both flat work and jumping.

What happened in the process of streamlining the Renaissance saddle was that the tree, departing from the 'howdah' principle, was made longer and somewhat flatter so as to follow the line of the back. For the purpose of riding across country, the high supporting rolls at the cantle and fore-arch of the *selle royale*, suitable for the *manège*, would have been dangerously confining – a certain freedom in the seat's adjustment is vital when negotiating a variety of fences at even a moderate pace.

The stirrup bars, always the villain of the piece, were, in the hunting saddle, fastened just below the juncture of the frame with the fore-arch, on the top of the 'point' (the extension of the fore-arch below the side-bars), a further rivet securing the top of the bar to the arm of the tree. Despite a slight forward swell of the flap and panel, the former often incorporating a built-in roll at its front edge, the bar was *too far forward* in relation to the saddle's shape. Inevitably, if the fore-arch was to stand well clear of the wither, the saddle sat higher in front than behind. In consequence, the rider was pushed somewhat towards the cantle and, because of the position of the stirrup bar, found it easier to sit with his lower leg forward and his weight behind the movement, and that still happened even if there was some dip to the seat. Indeed, even when the seat was dipped a little, as most of them were, its deepest part was positioned too far to the rear of the tree.

None the less, the English hunters were fit, strong and, by temperament, well suited to work across country. They were also ridden by bold, natural horsemen of no mean ability. It is pretty certain that these thrusting foxhunters would have been quite out of their depth in Europe's baroque riding halls, but in open country they were in their element and unbeatable. Moreover, while they rode in potentially severe double bridles, they appreciated to the full the need for 'good hands' and although they leant back at their fences, they did not interfere with their horses' mouths.

Saddles, not much altered from those in vogue throughout the nineteenth century, were still in regular use and were being made in England 20 years after the Second World War. (Indeed, in the late 1950s I still had a London-made polo saddle on which my grandfather had played in the early 1880s; but then I still have a pair of my father's field boots, made in Simla, India, in 1923.)

For a long time, hunting saddles and polo saddles were made with a full panel, the lower part following the shape of the flap and being quilted by spot stitching. Later, largely because of the influence of polo players based at what was then the popular polo centre of Rugby, the lower part of the panel was dispensed with, so that there was less bulk under the rider's leg. This half-panel was known as a Rugby panel or, less correctly, a Whippy panel, Whippy being the name of the London firm that specialised in panels of this shape.

2: The Military Saddle

It was during the nineteenth century that much detailed attention was given to the principles of saddle fitting and construction by possibly no more than a handful of enthusiastic 'professional' cavalry officers. The distinction is made because professionalism, as opposed to reckless bravery, in the mounted arms was not much in evidence until towards the end of the century and the standard of horsemastership, which had been high under commanders like Charles XII, Marlborough and Frederick II of Prussia, was sometimes appallingly low as a result.

Napoleon suffered enormous horse wastage in all his campaigns, losing some 30,000 animals in his abortive attempt to take Moscow. Nearly 50 years later, the French had still not learnt the lesson. At the battle of Solferino in 1859, the French cavalry complement amounted to 10,206, but no more than 3,500 horses were fit enough to be put in the field. In the South African War (the Boer War) the British lost 326,000 horses out of 494,000 berween 1899 and 1902, but only a few as a result of enemy action. The officer heading the subsequent enquiry, General Brabazon, pronounced it a 'shameful abuse of horse flesh'. The British did learn, however, and maintained impeccable standards up to the time cavalry regiments gave up their horses in favour of tanks and armoured vehicles in 1939–40. In the opening stages of the First World War, a conflict that involved millions of horses, only the British cavalry formations remained operational. Both the German and French mounted arms were rendered almost impotent by horse casualties resulting from what amounted to incompetent horse-management.

Enormous wastage resulted from ill-fitting saddles, a fact

recognised by one of the most articulate of the nineteenth-century cavalry reformers, Francis Dwyer, a professional soldier employed as a 'Major of Hussars in the Imperial Austrian Service'. (A number of such officers, younger sons without the means to take commissions in British cavalry regiments, and often of Anglo-Irish descent, served in the forces of the hugely sprawling Austro-Hungarian Empire; the Indian regiments, too, attracted the same sort of men and for the same reasons. Louis Edward Nolan, famous as the officer who carried the message that resulted in the disastrous charge of the Light Brigade at Balaclava in 1854, was just such a man, having begun his career in the Austrian service, to which the Hungarian cavalry was integral. In fact, Nolan, who was killed just as the charge began, was far and away the most outstanding cavalry officer of his generation and he, like Dwyer, devoted much time and energy to the design and maintenance of cavalry saddles.)

Following the Crimean War, much work was done to produce an effective saddle for cavalry. The result was the Universal Pattern saddle, constructed to Nolan's recommendations and based on the Hungarian light cavalry saddle – the Hungarian hussars, descendants of the steppe horsemen of Asia, were without doubt the light cavalrymen of the world *par excellence*.

The U.P. saddle survives today in its essentials and is the basis for all European cavalry saddles. Initially, the saddle was called the Nolan saddle and it would have been appropriate if the name had been retained as a memorial to the most advanced cavalry thinker of his time, whose only failing was 'a great excess of enthusiasm'.

The American cavalry, unfettered by the dictates of sumptuous ceremonial, produced its own version of the Hungarian saddle, the McClellan, which owes just as much as the U.P. to Louis Nolan.

In general, American troopers were far better practical horsemen than their counterparts in Europe, other than the Hungarians.

Moyse-Bartlett, Nolan's biographer (*Louis Edward Nolan and his influence on the British Cavalry*, Leo Cooper, 1971), wrote of Nolan that, 'The efficient state of the British cavalry at Balaclava was mainly attributed to his skill; after his death the horses were "allowed to die of hunger and for want of shelter".'

The McClellan saddle, different from the basic Hungarian saddle only in respect of detail and the addition of Western-style stirrups and cinches, was a horseman's saddle and not overcomfortable or suitable for a novice. It consisted of two arches, joined by side-bars that carried pads, the seat being a piece of rawhide stretched between the arches. It was very light, no more than 2–2·5 kg (5–6 lb), in contrast to the 6–8 kg (15 lb) of the U.P. saddle, and was worn over a blanket. The saddle was brought from Hungary in 1858 by the future General George B. McClellan and was in service up to 1940.

Dwyer produced his 'new and enlarged edition' of *Seats and Saddles, Bits and Bitting, Draught and Harness* in 1869. In it he defined the principles of saddle fitting with a clarity that has yet to be exceeded.

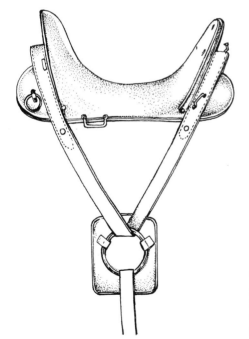

The American McClellan saddle based on the Hungarian pattern. It was very light and not very comfortable

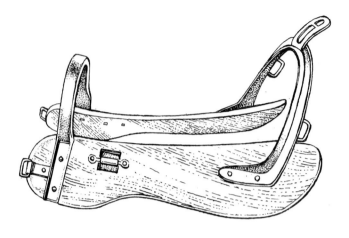

(*Above*) The tree of the Army Universal Pattern (U.P.) saddle. (*Opposite*) The completed U.P. saddle which was derived largely from Louis Nolan's recommendations and is still in service throughout the world. The saddle could be repaired with no more than a screwdriver, a knife and a piece of twine!

His principal concern, and Nolan's too, was to keep large numbers of horses fit for service in the field, while taking into account that most nineteenth-century cavalrymen would be indifferent horsemen. For that to be accomplished it was necessary, other aspects of management apart, to devise a saddle that could be adjusted, if only by the use of a blanket, to fit a variety of horses (many of them no more than the roughest of remounts) when they were employed under active service conditions.

In the field, where horses and men carrying full equipment were likely to undertake forced marches, subsisting on the feedstuffs that came to hand, the horses were bound to lose at least some of their original condition, the shape of the back changing as a result. The same thing happens when a fat hunter is brought up from grass. In the metamorphosis from fatness to fitness, surplus flesh is lost and the saddle that was adequate in

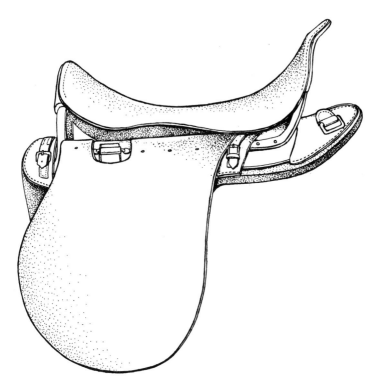

late summer may be much less so – even to the point when it causes damage by galling – during the following February, March and April, when the season draws to a close.

While the horse's well-being was paramount – as a dismounted cavalryman is not much use in the fulfilment of the role of the mounted arm – it was also necessary that the saddle should position a rider of no more than average competence, who might, additionally, be tired as a result of his exertions, in such a way that he would maintain a balanced seat without excessive effort. If the weight was carried correctly, it would allow the horse, which might be equally fatigued, to move freely without the inhibition caused by misplaced weight interfering with its natural balance and adding unnecessarily to the effort it was required to make. A matter of the utmost importance, of course, was to ensure that the weight, apart from its correct positioning in relation to the framework of the horse, was equally distributed over the largest available bearing surface, so as to obviate the possibility of pressure points arising from a concentration of weight over a limited area.

Dwyer continued '. . . as regards shape, the under side of the saddle should bear as nearly as possible the same relation to that part of the horse's back as it is intended to occupy, *as a mould does to the cast that is taken from it, always saving and excepting that strip lying over the horse's backbone which must remain altogether out of contact.*' (The italics are mine.) Was there ever so succinct an exposition of the saddle/back relationship?

Dwyer calculated that the optimum point over which the rider should be positioned was the fourteenth dorsal vertebra, which he described as being the 'keystone of the arch' – the spinal processes of the first 13 vertebrae, from the point of the neck's attachment, are inclined backwards, while vertebrae 15–18 and the six lumbar vertebrae incline forwards. Only the fourteenth stands upright. He argued that the fourteenth vertebra represents the *centre of motion of the horse's body* (not to be confused with the centre of gravity which will shift according to the speed and outline adopted and will, indeed, move sideways in lateral movements).

The conditions, as enumerated by Dwyer, were, in his view, met by the Hungarian light cavalry saddle, which was not that much different from a type used by the Huns, the forebears of the Hungarians. Originally, it was made entirely of wood without any metal reinforcement. Dwyer admitted that it might break, 'but it could be repaired or a new one made at the side of a ditch, and in time for the next day's march'. (The basic repair kit recommended for the U.P. saddle was a piece of twine, a knife and a screwdriver.)

Dwyer had this to say about contemporary saddles, although one suspects it might have been too much of a generalisation: 'We 19th century men have improved it everywhere [i.e. the Hungarian saddle], especially in England, up to more than double its original weight, to a total incapacity for repair or alteration, and to being the most efficient instrument conceivable for making holes in horses' backs.' (I can think of some modern saddles to which that stricture might in part still apply.)

The Hungarian saddle, which Dwyer held should fit the man

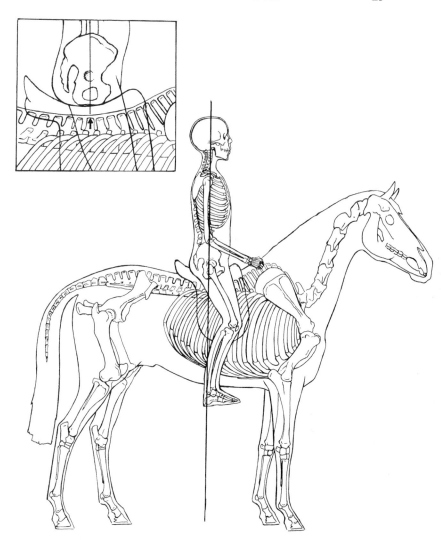

The saddle fitting the horse to perfection; placing the rider centrally over Dwyer's *centre of motion*, the fourteenth vertebra. It should be noted, however, that the horse is exceptionally well made. Horses whose conformation is less good cannot by their nature carry either saddle or rider so well or so comfortably. It is easy to see that the saddle cannot possibly impinge upon the movement of the scapula (the shoulder blade)

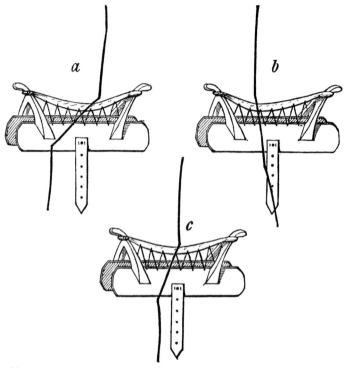

The Hungarian cavalry saddle. Position *a* shows the effect of lacing the seat so that the lowest point is too far to the rear. The opposite fault is demonstrated in Position *b*. Position *c* shows the correct lacing positioning the rider centrally. In this ultimate light cavalry saddle it was possible, as the diagram makes clear, to achieve a very precise adjustment

as well as the horse if the principles relative to the fitting of the latter's back were to be obtained, was as simple as it was effective.

Essentially it comprised two wooden bars, the angle of which could be adjusted to a degree and which joined wooden arches at the front and rear. Between the latter was stretched a 'bearing strap', laced to the bars on either side, the seat being covered with canvas.

It was as necessary, wrote Dwyer, 'to make the saddle fit the man's seat, as to make his coat or boots fit his body or feet'. By shortening or lengthening the bearing strap of the seat, or by altering the lacings, it was possible to position the rider centrally in accordance with his conformation.

The stirrup leathers were placed directly under the rider, as with the horse-archers of antiquity, as in that position they kept the seat central and supported a secure platform from which a man could use his weapons to the greatest effect. Furthermore, as Dwyer made clear, stirrups so placed make it very much more difficult for the rider to fall off sideways.

A footnote in Dwyer's chapter on saddles reads as follows: 'Any defects that may exist in the English cavalry seat, and the very glaring ones that are obvious in the French seat, and were the immediate causes of all the sore backs in the campaign of 1859, depend on the wrong position of the stirrup in the respective military saddles.' (The Nolan saddle had yet to come into general use at that time.)

Dwyer summarised the general rule as being: 'The saddle in the centre of the horse's back; the girths, stirrups and rider in the centre of the saddle.'

Like the spartan McClennan saddle, the Hungarian pattern had no heavy leather flap between the horse and the rider's leg, allowing, as Dwyer says, for 'the leg to be wrapped round the horse and in contact with two-thirds of its length', a surprisingly modern observation.

The studies made by Dwyer, Nolan and one or two of their contemporaries remain absolutely relevant insofar as the principles for the fitting of the horse's back are concerned. Furthermore, the saddles they advocated were entirely aligned to the needs of cavalry in the context of the time. Indeed, the U.P. saddle remains in use in countries all over the world and it still provides an excellent basis for the production of a distance riding saddle.

However, equestrian theory and practice, like almost everything else, are subject to change (although not so much as we might sometimes think). Dwyer's Hungarian saddle, Nolan's Universal Pattern and the US Army's McClellan would not meet the requirements of the present-day competition rider in the showjumping arena and on the cross-country course. Jumping

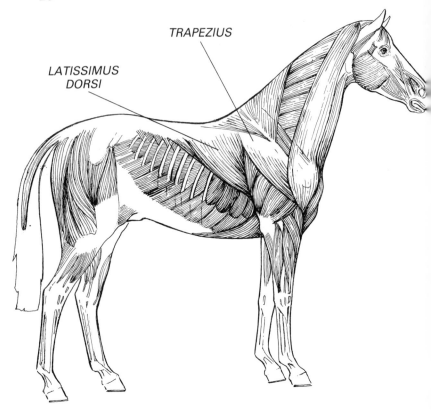

TRAPEZIUS

LATISSIMUS DORSI

The musculature of the well-proportioned horse allows the saddle to sit behind the big trapezius muscle

is, indeed, barely mentioned by Dwyer and what references there are reveal how little consideration he gave to the practice, but then cavalry manoeuvring on the Hungarian *puszta* (plain) were not required to jump, had there, indeed, been anything to jump, nor in any other part of the world at that time could one have imagined cavalry jumping by squadrons!

The subsequent development of the civilian saddle came about as a result of the innovatory theories propounded by an Italian cavalry officer, Captain Federico Caprilli (1868–1907). His theories, representing almost a revolution in equestrian history, turned accepted practice on its head and even, in the end, compelled a rethink about the position of that tiresome stirrup bar.

3: Caprilli the Innovator

Every so often in the human progression there occurs a landmark of particular importance – a watershed dividing one era from the next. In the equestrian context, domestication of the horse was just such a landmark. The works of Xenophon, written in the third century BC, contained instruction on training horses based on an understanding of the equine nature. They were unique in their range and depth; rediscovered, they acted as an inspiration for the classical art of the Renaissance, and they remain, in many respects, a relevant influence within the modern horse world.

The invention of the stirrup extended and altered forever the ways in which men would use horses, while the Renaissance itself and the subsequent expansion of riding as a rational science (rather than an instinctive accomplishment) was an advance of the greatest magnitude.

Even so, the principles of classicism had become largely debased, so far as sporting pursuits and active military requirement were concerned, as early as the end of the sixteenth century. None the less, instruction at the nineteenth-century cavalry schools continued to be based on the *manège* riding of the seventeenth and eighteenth centuries, the accent being placed on collection at slow paces. It suited the parade ground movement of cavalry well enough and it made possible the manoeuvring of large bodies of horse in open country. Jumping formed little or no part of basic cavalry instruction, which was probably as well for such early pictures as exist are little short of horrific – horses jumping hollow-backed, their heads thrown up to avoid in some measure the discomfort imposed by the rider's ungiving hand, a hand held somewhere about chest height.

Dwyer, who wrote so well about saddles and was meticulous

in his study of the principles of bitting, is reticent when it comes to jumping. Indeed, the short passage he includes seems to be advocating a method 'to insure [*sic*] his [i.e. the horse] landing on all four feet instead of two only'.

What the cavalry instructors, and particularly the generals, would not or could not recognise was that increasingly effective fire-power radically altered the traditional role of cavalry. The 'cavalry spirit' was all very well, but the set-piece charge of squadrons in line – to which cavalry training was largely directed – was hardly viable when opposed by machine-guns and the rapid-fire capability of modern rifles.

Federico Caprilli, born in Leghorn in 1868, the son of a well-to-do Tuscan family, became an instructor at Tor di Quinto, an adjunct of the principal Italian cavalry school at Pinerolo, in 1894, and was subsequently chief instructor at Pinerolo. He died in December 1907 in Turin when he appeared to faint while riding at a walk, falling from his horse and suffering severe head injuries.

In his short life, however, Caprilli altered the whole concept of cross-country riding and jumping. At a distance of some 90 years it is difficult for a generation well accustomed to seeing riders sitting forward at their fences to appreciate the magnitude of his accomplishment. In fact, his theories caused almost as much outcry in military circles as Charles Darwin's explanation of evolution, propounded in *The Origin of the Species by Means of Natural Selection*, had done among the religious leaders of the day. This book, published in 1835, was viewed by the Church in much the same light as the Muslim hierarchy now regard Salman Rushdie's *Satanic Verses* and from pulpits throughout the land clerics thundered mightily against what they saw as an outrageous blasphemy. Caprilli was just as unpopular with the generals, who condemned his theories with irrational violence and even forbade their practice.

A diligent and far-seeing student of cavalry tactics, in the same mould as the Englishman Nolan, whom he resembled in temperament, Caprilli was quick to appreciate the changing role of cavalry. He saw it as a swiftly moving screen for the flanks of the main body, which could also probe forward to discover the enemy dispositions. It was to act as the eyes of the army as a

Federico Caprilli in 1904 when the forward system was still developing

reconnaissance arm and, finally, it could be used to exploit a breakthrough in the enemy line.

To fulfil that function it was obviously necessary for mounted detachments to be able to move across country swiftly, negotiating whatever obstacles lay in their path. Increasingly, there were more such obstacles – fences, ditches, banks, etc. – as land enclosures became more commonplace.

It was just as obvious that European cavalry, schooled in collected paces within the *manège*, were ill-fitted in every way to fulfil this essentially light cavalry role. It was not so much that they leaned backwards as that they thought backwards also.

Caprilli's declared intent, and the basis for *il sistema*, was to abolish the 'school' methods, which he eventually succeeded in doing at Pinerolo, and to replace them with a 'natural' system of riding, where schooling was carried out largely in the country-side, on the very terrain, in fact, over which cavalry might be expected to operate. Jumping over artificial fences was part of the schooling, but for Caprilli it was a means to an end and of academic interest. He saw *il sistema* 'as a means of getting cavalry across a country with the least possible strain on both men and horses'.

Discarding the *manège* and its ideal of the completely controlled horse, he schooled horses to move in unfettered extension, carrying the head and neck naturally and adapting their balance according to the ground. Instead of the rider insisting, via the system of levers and curb bits, on the horse conforming in respect of outline and carriage to the dictates of the hand – a form that was in itself unnatural – he required his *riders* to conform instead to the horse's natural movement and outline.

Horses trained in this way found their own balance and developed initiative on their own account. If the rider's weight was positioned forward in line with the horse's centre of balance, and the hand was advanced, rather than being withdrawn, the loins were at once freed and the horse would be able to jump without interference, as in nature, i.e. with rounded back and head and neck lowered and extended.

Caprilli's system is often considered to be one of supreme non-intervention, but that is a misconception if not interfering with the balance is confused with passivity. In movement, the Caprilli-trained horse was required to remain at an even pace, which is not within the ability of the passive rider. On the Tor di Quinto training grounds, where the country was undulating and the track lay over banks, fences, ditches and some fearsome slide obstacles, riders were expected to keep a distance of two lengths between the horses and maintain this position through-out the ride.

This seat, which became known as the *forward seat*, a mistaken nomenclature, for it was in reality only the outward manifestation of a principle, called for a shorter leather if the

(*Above and below*) The jumping seat before Caprilli . . . and (*opposite*) after

rider was to adjust his body weight forward in accordance with
the horse's centre of balance. In the early days of the Caprilli
system, it is noticeable that riders were often too upright in the
body with the lower leg unsufficiently drawn back. This was the
result of three hundred years of *manège*-dominated riding, but
it was also on account of the saddle design, which in many
instances opposed the adoption of the true Caprilli seat, largely
through the position of the stirrup bar. Once the saddles, like
those made in Italy by Pariani, conformed more nearly to the
new theory of forward riding, the seat over fences came closer
to the ideal, but it certainly did not happen overnight, despite
the success of Italian teams in international competition.
Caprilli's system was given impetus by the growing interest in

arena jumping competition and in 'the military', the name under which eventing was known. His teachings were accepted and practised not only in Italy, where they erected a Caprilli Cenotaph in his memory at Tor di Quinto, but by the cavalry establishments of other nations as well.

Without any doubt, the influence of the Caprilli principle dominates modern riding, particularly in respect of arena jumping and, to a considerable degree, in regard to cross-country riding also, but, in fact, his system, involving the outright rejection of the classical *manège* training, was not adopted in its entirety. For the most part, the world has effected a compromise, a blending of the classical with the Caprilli system, while retaining the latter's ideals of forward movement, something that was in danger of being lost within the too-rigid military systems of the latter half of the nineteenth century. In Britain, the cavalry school at Weedon developed the 'balanced seat' which reflected the British cross-country tradition and was to characterise British riding between the two world wars and after.

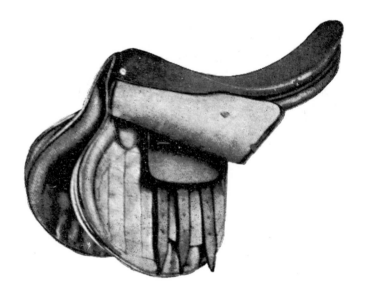

A pre-war Italian saddle by Pariani made on a spring tree

Whether Caprilli would have continued to develop his theories can only be a matter for conjecture. He left no more than some brief notes, never attempting a detailed exposition that might have formed a basis for further study. For the most part, his work was interpreted to the world in books and articles by his pupil and disciple Major Piero Santini, who was responsible, in the 1930s, for the design of the Santini saddle, an item made up in the saddlery town of Walsall, England, and which was claimed to conform to Caprilli's system.

Between the two world wars the altered pattern of riding produced a variety of saddles more or less designed to assist the rider's position, and increased use was made of the now ubiquitous spring tree, particularly in the saddles of mainland Europe, like those produced in Milan by Pariani.

Walsall, undeniably the centre of the world's saddlery and horse furniture industry up to the 1960s, lays claim to the invention of the spring tree before the turn of the century. The matter is open to argument, but what is certain is that Walsall did not promote the product until after the Second World War,

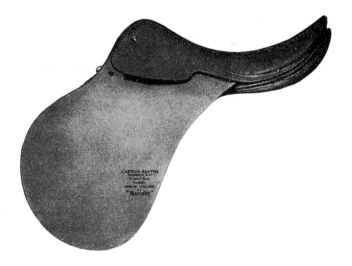

A Santini saddle, designed by Piero Santini and made in Walsall by Barnsby

whereas it was in relatively general use elsewhere in Europe at least a quarter of a century previously. (A spring tree has two strips of tempered steel laid lengthways from behind the head [fore-arch] to the cantle, so as to give resilience to the seat.)

4: Between the Wars

As a result of Caprilli's teaching and its influence on the cavalry schools, which continued to dominate equestrian thinking up to the Second World War, the design of saddles began to change to accommodate the new requirement. Further encouragement was given by the growth in national and international sporting competition, even though participation, certainly in the latter, was confined almost entirely to the military.

Equestrian events were first included at the 1912 Stockholm Olympics; the *Fédération Équestre Internationale* (FEI), the world governing body for the three Olympic disciplines of dressage, jumping and horse trials, as the sport has come to be known, was founded in 1921; the British Show Jumping Association, formed to create, from chaos, a set of rules for the national sport, came into being two years later. The British Pony Club, which was to become the biggest association of riders in the world, started in 1929. A relative newcomer is the British Horse Society which was formed in 1947 as a result of the amalgamation of the National Horse Association of Great Britain (1923) and the Institute of the Horse (1925), a body into which the Pony Club was later incorporated.

In Europe, where hunting was less integral to the equestrian scene, the saddles of the period reflected the greater interest in competitive sport. Of course, Pariani, in Milan, was making a jumping saddle on a spring tree soon after the end of the First World War, while the French saddles, often made by Hermès in Paris, used a 'Saumur' panel incorporating supportive forward rolls. The design of these saddles owed much to Colonel Danloux, commandant at Saumur, and were often made with triangular 'squabs' on the rear of the sweat flap, which fitted

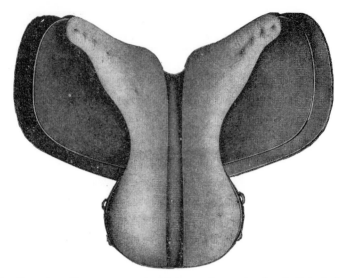

The French or Saumur panel which was in production in Britain from the late 1920s

into the crook of the rider's knee and assisted in the maintenance of the leg position.

It was possible in the 1930s to buy Pariani saddles in Britain, and also the French patterns, but for the most part the British rode in order to hunt, rather than compete, as they had done for two hundred years, and even the Pony Club branches were firmly attached to their local packs, as, indeed, most of them still are today. Hacking was probably a more popular diversion than it is now, but then there were plenty of bridleways on which to ride and traffic was minimal in comparison to the volume we are experiencing in the last decade of the twentieth century.

There were, of course, plenty of horse shows, including the splendid International under its presiding genius, Lord Lonsdale.

Dressage, however, was barely understood and was practised by no more than a handful of riders. There was showjumping on an unimaginably small scale, but because of the rules, or the lack of them (time, for instance, was not involved), it was for the most part a boring, uninspired exercise that attracted no popular following despite the performances of some brilliant civilian riders. In the years leading up to the Second World War many county shows did not stage a jumping competition at all, and that was the case at the last Royal which was held at Lincoln before the outbreak of war in 1939.

None the less, a discernible ground swell of interest and enquiry, having almost a Renaissance quality about it, arose within the British horse world and spanned the brief 20-odd years between the two world wars. At its base were the instructors and past instructors of the cavalry schools at Weedon and at Saugur in India and it was made very evident in the content of the leading magazine of its day, *Riding*, originally edited by R. S. Summerhays. The monthly paper became a forum for the most eminent equestrian writers of the time: Henry Wynmalen, Jack Hance, Barrowcliff-Ellis, Phil Blackmore, Faudel-Phillips, Piero Santini (the pupil of Caprilli), F. E. Gibson, the horseman turned saddler, and a whole lot more. (*Horse and Hound* then, as now, a weekly newspaper, was the world leader, but its purpose was the dissemination of news combined with comment. In those days it did not presume to mount an instructional platform.)

A perusal of the early issues of *Riding* reveals clearly the equestrian interest of the time, while the advertisement columns are equally valuable in tracing the development of ideas and equipment.

With some concessions to the advancement of equestrian theory, notably in the more forward cut of flap and panel, the English hunting saddle remained predominant. The bars, however, were fixed in much the same place and did nothing to help the rider conform to the horse's movement. At this time, too, there was a rash of safety bars designed to release the leather in the event of a fall. In the previous century there had been even more (upwards of 25 patterns); today no bars of this type are manufactured in Britain at all. On the whole, despite the ingenuity displayed in their construction, they do not seem to have been very popular and few, if any, of the experts supported their use, most preferring to put their trust in a good, heavy iron.

Interestingly, there was much concern with a proper fitting of the saddle and a far greater awareness of the horse's comfort. To ensure trouble-free fitting, various types of panel were recommended. There was the Wykeham, which depended on the insertion of shaped pieces of felt; another was less than grammatically termed the 'Loose Saddle Panel' and was slotted on to the tree, and there was also a panel constructed of sorbo rubber, a forerunner of today's plastics. This latter was only effective to a point, as it tended to overheat and could even scald the back. Today's almost indispensable numnah was notably absent in the tack rooms of the period, which says something for the fit of the saddles and the standard of horse-management – both, perhaps, were better appreciated than is the case today.

In terms of quality no saddle in the world compared with those made in Britain, especially the products of the London saddlers whose names were household words well beyond their native shores. For craftsmanship and the superlative quality of the materials used, there was no exceeding the mainly bespoke products of Owen, Whippy, Champion and Wilton, Sowter and one or two more, but for all that the Walsall, wholesale, off-the-peg product was not far behind.

Saddles of that time, whether made in London or Walsall, were uniformly 'London' colour (a light, yellowish tan) and most of the bridlework was of the same hue. Properly cared for, it toned down to wonderful shades of rich mahogany, far superior to the aniline-dressed dark brown tans and the stained black leathers that are popular now.

The craftsmen of Walsall, while possessed of great ingenuity, were hardly avant-garde in terms of design, but then neither were the élite of the trade in London. None the less, the advances that occurred in the design of British saddles came from Walsall and the most significant innovations in the design of saddle trees and saddles made following the Second World War, emanated from the same predominantly conservative source. (That developments in modern equestrian equipment seem to take so unconscionable a time to come about is due largely to the fact that the tree-maker and the saddle-maker, who belong to quite separate trades – and the bridle-maker, too – very rarely have any connection with the horse and the varied purposes to which it is put. Mind you, that doesn't say much for the innovative instinct or communicative power of the horseman either.)

The two most notable departures from the conventional hunting, showing and polo patterns from 1918–39 were the Santini saddle, made by Barnsby, and the Distas Central Position saddle.

Piero Santini, as we know, was the pupil of Caprilli, and the saddle he made in Walsall in the 1930s must, one supposes, have been designed in accordance with the principles expounded by the Master. It was, indeed, close in some of its details to the Toptani pattern so successfully marketed by Messrs Parker from the 1950s onwards. On the whole, it does not seem to have had the impact that might have been expected. Possibly, having a 'parchment' tree (a resilient tree), it was still too far advanced for the very effective, talented, balanced-seat horsemen of Weedon. They were happy enough to adapt their hunting saddles, enlarging the forward inclination of flap and panel but doing little about the relationship of the latter to the seat or, once more, the critical placing of the stirrup bar.

The Distas saddle, on the other hand, was more acceptable to the British riding public, largely because its line was less extreme. It was made to the design of Lieutenant-Colonel F. E. Gibson following, it is said, a conversation between him and Lieutenant-Colonel Jack Hance.

After the First World War, in which Gibson had served with distinction, this member of a prominent banking family indulged his passion for horses, eventually setting up a dealing yard. From that, after a sojourn in America, he founded the saddlery firm of Distas in London, the name arising because he also had, at the time, an agency for the sale of stable disinfectant.

Hance, who, as a rough-riding sergeant, had instructed Gibson at St John's Wood, became one of Britain's great instructors and a legendary character. He was among the first of his generation to appreciate the value of dressage and attended the European schools regularly. Before the Second World War his establishment at Malvern was world famous and from there he turned out a host of very expert riders.

He and Gibson worked and did business together. One day, so the story goes, Hance complained that he could not get pupils to sit correctly in civilian saddles because the shape of the tree (and the forward position of the bars?) placed them towards the cantle and behind the movement. He had, he said, only one saddle that actually helped the rider to sit correctly. It was an old Australian-style stock saddle and, as it turned out, it had a broken tree, which was why the rider could sit so easily in its centre. Gibson, who had already published 'Notes on "Dipped" Saddles' among a series of articles for the magazine *Riding*, had for some years been interested in the Australian stock saddle, a thoroughly practical piece of equipment for hard-riding stock hands accustomed to long hours on horseback. It had, and still has, for it remains in general use, features that were the fruit of long experience, among which was a dipped seat and a narrow 'twist' or waist that prevented the spreading of the upper thighs.

Gibson took away Hance's old saddle and built one with a similarly dipped seat but less exaggerated in the forward sweep of the panel than the Santini model. It was immediately popular, but then the Second World War began and both he and Hance returned to the forces, leaving all thoughts of saddles in abeyance for the duration.

None the less, Santini's saddle, the imported Parianis, the Saumur patterns and one or two copies of those marques, along with the Distas, had paved the way for a later and much more significant development. (The Walsall-made Saumur patterns were greatly superior to the French saddles in respect of the tree, the materials used and the workmanship.)

At the outbreak of war, with the exception of the military saddles, which were manufactured in large quantities for export, and some specialised models like the American Walking Horse saddle, Walsall production was largely concerned with the following saddles.

Hunting

These were made either with full or half (Rugby) panels. Both might be wool-stuffed and covered with leather or, as was

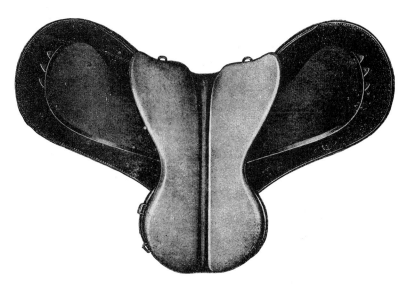

(*Above*) The English Rugby or half-panel; (*below*) the panel from which Toptani created his jumping saddle. Note how it narrows significantly at the waist

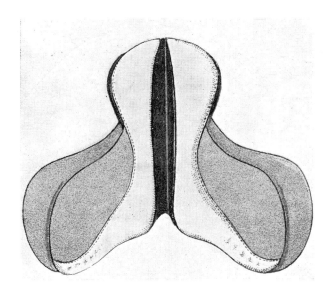

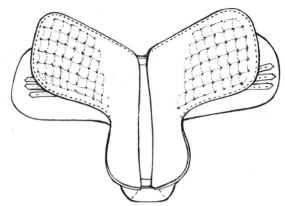

The full panel was still fitted to hunting saddles after the Second World War and indeed well into the 1950s

frequent, with wool serge over which linen was often laid. The linen prevented the serge from becoming impossibly dirty and also prevented undue absorption of sweat into the wool stuffing. The advantage of a serge lining was the ease with which the wool stuffing could be adjusted to the back by a competent saddler. (In pre-war days it was not unusual for a saddler to visit a large yard so as to be able to adjust the saddle fittings on the spot.)

Hunting saddles might also be made up with leather-covered panels made of felt, and this was almost always the case when a Saumur panel was used. The advantage of a felt panel (when made in Walsall, but not in France) was that it gave a closer fit to the back and also allowed the rider to be that much closer to the horse. The fit could not, of course, be adjusted so easily, although a layer of wool was placed on the bearing side of the panel.

Polo Saddles

These were built on extra strong trees and were almost always made with Rugby panels.

Show Saddles

These, too, had short panels; usually, but not always, covered in

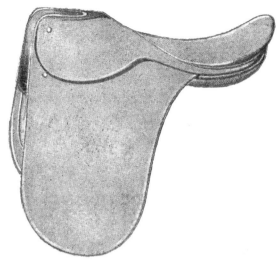

Conventional, straight-cut show saddle made on a felt half-panel

leather. The saddle was made to fit close so as not to interrupt the line of the back, and the flap was cut pretty well straight – to persuade the judge, one supposes, that the horse was possessed of an even bigger front than was truly the case.

Jumping Saddles

There were, of course, jumping saddles other than those already mentioned. Most, however, were no more than variations on the hunting saddle, being cut a little further forward, while some jumpers used what was to all intents a steeplechasing saddle or even the race-exercise saddle of the training yard. The panels on these saddles were always of the full pattern. They reappeared, half a century later, as the so-called 'close contact' saddles, to be hailed as the ultimate in jump saddle design. (A favourite with showjumpers, particularly in Australia where it originated, was Bartley's patent Cobbar saddle, first made for the British market in London and later in Walsall. It was a substantial, but none the less very light, all-felt saddle, built with a channel to ensure that no pressure was put on the spine, and it was comfortable for both horse and rider – a steppe horseman of the pre-Christian era would have been entirely at home on it!)

Saddles were made up on beechwood trees, reinforced with steel gullet plates, etc., and were available, probably unnecessarily, in a greater variety of lengths, widths and shapings than is the case today.

Despite Walsall's dubious claim to have introduced the spring tree in the latter part of the nineteenth century, few, if any, trees of this type were in use, although Gibson was beginning to have them made for the Distas immediately before the outbreak of war in 1939.

5: Town of a Hundred Trades

Fifty years after the Industrial Revolution, which might be considered to occupy the years between 1789–1832, the Midland town of Walsall was, indeed, beginning to see itself as the 'Town of a Hundred Trades' and was becoming established as a world centre for the production of saddlery, harness, lorinery and the legion of metal fittings, clips, dees, buckles and squares that comprise horse 'furniture'.

Walsall also supported industries as diverse as organ-making and spectacle and false teeth manufacturing, claiming in this last respect that: 'The whole world is the customer of the artificial teeth experts of Walsall'! From the sixteenth century onwards, however, its staple, traditional industry had been horse equipment and well into the twentieth century it was the principal supplier of horse accoutrements for the cavalry, police forces and horse transport of the British Empire, with strong markets in countries outside that vast conglomerate, particularly in North America.

Following the Second World War, even though some of its traditional trade outlets were in decline, Walsall benefited, at least initially, from the remarkable surge of growing interest in the horse in Britain and elsewhere. The old social barriers had crumbled under the levelling influence of six years of wartime conditions. This new society had both money and leisure time as never before. Riding and horse ownership, until then the virtual prerogative of country people and the upper classes, became, increasingly, the recreation of urban and suburban dwellers. Television popularised horse sports by taking showjumping into millions of homes and, in consequence, the call for Walsall products, particularly when the voracious American market was taken into account, approached a point where demand began to exceed the industry's ability to supply. It was a situation aggravated by various factors, not least the traditional 'cottage industry' character of the Walsall trade. None the less, up to the 1960s, when the town's position as a world-leader was coming under attack from a number of quarters, Walsall retained much of its reputation for quality and was in the forefront of saddle development. A principal innovator was Len Holmes, proprietor of the Walsall Riding Saddle Company. He laid the foundations for his company's fortunes by promoting his American export business and when, in the early 1950s, he collaborated with Count Ilias Toptani and F. E. Gibson, then connected with the London firm of George Parker, he made a major contribution to the future of the modern saddle and, indeed, may be said to have played a part in the altered concept of British competitive riding.

Holmes pioneered the Pli-bond tree, which was made in his own factory. The traditional tree originally had parts made by hand, from beechwood. The trees which Holmes made were constructed from strips of the same wood moulded with urea-formaldehyde resin. The result was a consistency in the shape and an end product that was both stronger (Holmes reinforced the wooden shape with lightweight steel or even Duralumin) and much lighter. Today, all modern trees follow this pattern and contructional technique.

6: Ilias Toptani

Count Ilias Toptani, a member of the Albanian royal family, visited Britain in the early 1950s, after the 1948 Olympics had been staged in London. A tall, very good-looking man, intelligent and highly articulate, he was possessed of great charm and charisma. He was a brilliant horseman in the pure Caprilli style, who had jumped internationally. He was also a trainer of exceptional ability, who had taught at riding centres worldwide, settling, if only temporarily, in South America where his teaching methods produced world-class teams that were certainly not mounted on horses of the calibre of the Americans and Europeans. (The Mexican team won the showjumping gold at the 1948 Olympics and its captain, Mariles Cortes, the individual gold medal.)

In his book *Modern Showjumping*, first published in 1954 and revised in 1972, Toptani describes in his typically fluent, racy style how he came to analyse saddle construction and design and then to build a saddle that actually improved the performance of horse and rider and, in the end, the standards of international jumping.

Like Jack Hance, Toptani became frustrated by riders who, whatever their talent, could not realise the potential that he knew they possessed. Also like Hance, he focused on the saddle, taking the best he had to Señor Pérez, 'seventh in a line of famous saddlers'. Pérez was affronted by the suggestion that anything could be wrong with one of his beautifully crafted saddles but agreed to accompany Toptani, with the saddle, to his riding club, where the Count had erected a jumping course of some 30 obstacles at a height of 1·5 m (5 ft).

Saddling his best jumper, Toptani invited Pérez to ride the course on the saddle he had made. That, of course, was impossible, for Pérez had only rarely been in touching distance of a horse and admitted so. It was, he declared, not his fault since he only built the saddle on the tree provided by his friend Señor Lôpez, the tree-maker. Forthwith, Toptani took the horse, the saddle and the saddler to the tree-maker who, Toptani reported, was so incensed that he reached for the knife he carried in his belt, telling Toptani to 'Go and have a few riding lessons'. When it was suggested that he should demonstrate by riding the horse over a few fences he, too, admitted that in all his life he had never sat on a horse. (When I told this story to a friend, this was his comment: 'If it wasn't for the names you could be talking about Walsall!')

Toptani, together with Señores Pérez and Lôpez, got down to building a saddle designed specifically for the purpose of competitive riding – or, indeed, for just riding. To do so Toptani returned to the saddles of the traditional horse-peoples, those that came out of Turkey, Mongolia and Arabia – the old steppe patterns, in fact. He built his saddle with a spring tree to give resilience in the seat, and he confirms that the first practical trees of this sort to find general acceptance were those used by Pariani in saddles built to conform with Caprilli's *il sistema* early on in the twentieth century.

When he came to Britain, the saddle he found nearest to his South American prototype was the Central-Position Distas and, once more, this time in conjunction with Holmes and Gibson, and with the co-operation of George Parker as the distributor, he set about the design of the saddle that was to bear his name and influence succeeding generations of British horsemen.

7: Toptani's Saddle

The saddle they produced was light, weighing only 4 kg (9 lb). It was built on a fairly dipped spring tree that was made deliberately narrow at the waist, so as not to spread the rider's thighs. Instead of being riveted onto the *outside* of the tree, on the point and the tree bar, the stirrup bars were recessed by the simple means of placing the bar on the *inside*. As a result, the bulk under the rider's thigh caused by bar and stirrup leather, was removed, allowing the thigh to rest flat on the saddle. For the same reason, but also out of consideration for the fitting of the back, the points below the stirrup bar were cut off short, ending in a piece of rounded flexible leather about 2·5–5 cm (1–2 in) long, that slotted into the point 'pockets' on the saddle panel. Flexible points, sometimes of rubber, had been used before but Toptani's attenuated point was particularly necessary on account of the tree's overriding feature, the angle of the fore-arch in relation to the vertical and the consequent positioning of the stirrup bar – that unsolved and unappreciated problem that had bedevilled the saddle for the best part of four hundred years.

In the conventional 'English' hunting saddle, the basis for so many of the European patterns, the bars had been too far forward in relation to the shape of the seat, which was flat and in which the dip, such as it was, placed the rider towards the cantle, behind the movement and the centre of balance, if not behind the very centre of movement itself.

The dip-seat of the Toptani saddle, designed, it must be remembered, specifically for jumping, positioned the rider much further forward and as close to the centre of balance as possible, while the panel was built to provide strong support in front of the knee for a rider using a shortened jumping-length

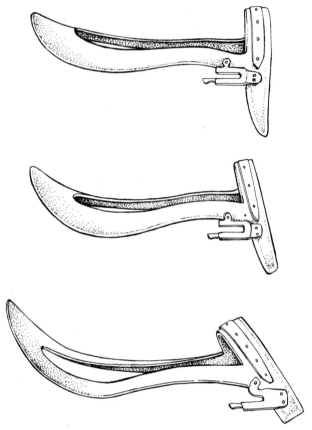

(*Top*) the conventional straight-headed tree of the English hunting saddle; (*centre*) the points sloped forward in the general purpose saddle to take the bars further to the front; (*below*) the sloped head on Toptani's jumping saddle

leather. To achieve that objective, however, it was necessary to think again about the critical positioning of the bar. In the conventional saddle the head, or fore-arch, was fitted vertically in relation to the body of the tree. Had that feature been retained in the Toptani saddle, with its dipped seat and forward-swept panels, the bar, instead of being too far forward, as in the hunting saddle, would have been just the opposite, i.e. it would have been *too far back* and as a result the rider would

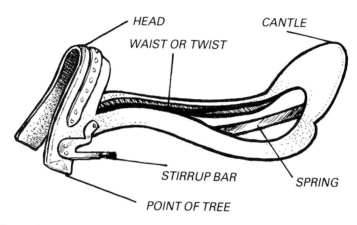

HEAD

WAIST OR TWIST

CANTLE

STIRRUP BAR

SPRING

POINT OF TREE

The spring tree, the springs set along the tree's length

have been quite unable to put his weight forward and over the stirrup iron while maintaining his anchoring leg position. The same would have applied if the head was of the cut-back variety, a device employed to give a greater range of fitting in respect of high wither formations.

The problem, after all those years when the bar had been placed too far to the front, was now, paradoxically, how to position it even further *forward*. The solution was to slope the head so that it joined the tree at an angle of 45 degrees. By doing this, the points were brought forward and with them the setting of the stirrup bar itself. Additionally, the sloped head was just as effective in relation to the fitting as the cut-back head, which, whatever its advantages, represents a weaker structure in the engineering sense.

The panel itself was built so as to present minimal bulk between the rider and his horse, and the narrowing of the tree at its waist, a line followed by the panel, contributed very materially to that end. Moreover, the saddle fitted very snugly ('as a mould does to the cast that is taken from it'), allowing the rider to sit close without being raised up off the back where his contact with the horse would be lessened.

A saddle allowing this sort of close contact lowered the rider's centre of gravity, therefore increasing the strength of the base. (Conversely, a heavily stuffed panel, broad at its waist and spreading the thighs, raises the rider away from the back, lifting the centre of gravity and reducing the strength of the base.)

To fulfil the principle of close contact more completely, Toptani had both the sweat flap and the flap itself made from leather of a very light substance (thickness). English saddles employed hard-wearing, heavy flap leather. It would last for upwards of 60 years, but only began to become supple during the lifetime of its third generation of owners. Durability of materials was a tenet of the saddler's faith, to be observed conscientiously but without reference to design and purpose, and the riding public expected, quite irrationally, a lifetime of service from their saddles, indeed, they wanted more than that, expecting to hand down a saddle from father to son to grandson.

Durability was not a priority in a precision instrument like Toptani's saddle, although it wore well enough and tree failures, under normal conditions, were unknown. In time, the thin flaps would show signs of wear and would rumple, but of what consequence was that? A new pair were easily enough fitted without in any way altering the design or detracting from the saddle's efficiency.

The springs of tempered steel, set longitudinally on the tree from head to cantle, added to the rider's comfort, giving a soft, resilient seat but, additionally, they increased the horse's comfort too, as they gave slightly to the movement of the back. (Only in later years did the spring tree create problems when corners were cut in cheaper copies. Seats were then allowed to take on an unnecessarily exaggerated dip and the steel 'springs' used were often of insufficient strength. As a result, the rider's weight was concentrated over an area so small as to produce pressure points midway down the back on either side.)

The Toptani saddle, like Caprilli's *il sistema*, to which it gave a renewed impetus, may not have been accepted universally but it altered forever the concept of saddle design and construction, established a principle (alas, not yet completely understood by either manufacturers or riders) and was instrumental in the

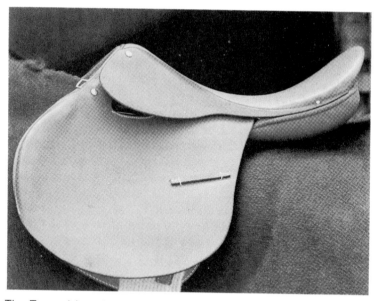

The Toptani jumping saddle designed by Count Ilias Toptani. The bars are inset to eliminate bulk under the thigh and the girth is positioned so that it lies behind the rider's leg

demise of the conventional English saddle – in fact, it put an end to it.

Of far greater import was the effect on the standard of British competitive riding, at both national and international levels, of a saddle that was a clear reflection of all the principles of forward riding over fences and in which it was possible to vindicate the teaching inherent in the Caprilli system.

Writing in the revised edition of *Modern Showjumping* in 1972, Toptani was able to state, with unusual modesty: '... I do now believe that the modern saddle I introduced to England, and which served as a pattern for many others, was partly instrumental in the great equestrian post-war successes of the British teams in international jumping events, and so were the modern methods as expounded in this book'. In hindsight, and having regard to the structure of the much smaller horse world of the time, there was justification for his claim.

Quite certainly, the Toptani was copied extensively by other makers and within a very short time a large part of the Walsall production was given over to saddles incorporating, more or less, the principles involved in its construction. Unhappily, as the manufacturers, almost to a man, were unable to appreciate those principles and had most certainly never thought of reading the book in which they were so clearly expounded, a lot of bad imitations came on the market.

In the light of developments in Walsall and in Europe over the past 20 years, and in particular within the last decade, it is worth recalling, in the interests of perspective, Toptani's assessments of the general saddle patterns with which he was familiar when he visited Britain in 1972.

In the 1954 publication of *Modern Showjumping* (then carrying the byline 'The South American Method'), he had effectively demolished the 'English'-pattern saddle while admitting that in terms of workmanship those made in England were 'the very finest in the world'. He administered the final *coup de grâce* in one devastating sentence: 'Hang your old saddles on the walls of your home as antiques – they might serve as a substitute for etchings.'

He was no more complimentary about the French saddles of the Danloux pattern, which unlike the English-made saddles, did not even have the saving grace of being well made.

In the 1972 revision Toptani had no need to discuss the 'English' saddle as it no longer existed, but he included critical commentaries on the French, German and Italian products.

About the French saddle, derived from Colonel Danloux's pattern, he remarked that many of the current patterns (i.e. of early 1970s vintage) would have made that 'excellent officer and successful horseman turn in his grave'. He went on to condemn 'the worst sort of French saddles' as having 'every single defect of all the other saddles made in Europe in earlier days and *none* of their very few good qualities'.

Toptani's criticism, which he acknowledged as being harsh, was based on the following shortcomings:

1   Weight – about 11 kg (25 lb);
2   Thick, stiff leather of poor quality;

3   Too broad between the rider's legs – 25 cm (10 in) wide in the waist as opposed to Toptani's 10 cm (4 in);

4   A weak front arch that spread after very little use, placing the rider in advance of the movement and thus overweighting the forehand;

5   Panels far too heavily stuffed, particularly at the cantle. As a result the rider sat *above* his horse rather than in contact, and the saddle's balance was seriously affected.

The criticism was certainly harsh, but it was no more severe than the product deserved.

Twenty years later some French saddles have improved, but they are still open to criticism, particularly on account of the trees used and the quality of the components.

The old-type German saddles received similarly short shrift (as did the style of the German riders of the period), but the modern patterns fared much better even though they employed then, as now, the largely irrational cut-back head. However, they were no longer heavy and were much narrower at the twist, while using soft, light leathers.

In 1972, Toptani did not think the German saddle either 'helpful' or 'entirely suitable' for jumping because of the still-apparent dressage influence. He attributed the German jumping successes to 'the outstanding quality of the superb German horses', which he regarded as being 'the finest types in the world for jumping'.

What is perhaps more relevant to the German saddle of the 1980s and 1990s is this comment: 'Surprisingly, the Germans, a conservative people, have a strong inclination towards fancy innovations and some of their products are so decorative that they look almost like a German version of the fancy Mexican parade saddles. But, perhaps, that is the influence of the American market.'

The Italian saddles, which without doubt drew largely on the design features of the Toptani, met, understandably, with more approval.

The Toptani is still made in Britain to this day and many would argue that it remains supreme as a jumping saddle. What has been lost in the flood of German pattern saddles that have dominated the market in recent years is the principle relative to the head and the position of the stirrup bar, which Toptani demonstrated so clearly.

8: The Head and the Bar

As we have seen, Toptani sloped the vertical head which had previously been used so as to take the bar further forward while obtaining the facility of the cut-back head. For the jumping saddle, in which a much shortened leather is used, Toptani's 45-degree slope was correct. However, for a saddle devoted to general purposes as, for instance, in the hunting field, when a rider is mounted for hours at a stretch and uses a somewhat longer leather, the slope of the head was too extreme. It needed to be reduced by about 15 degrees, when the forward sweep of panel and flap would be commensurately less exaggerated.

The Toptani was a jumping saddle, designed for the purpose of schooling over fences and for riding over an arena course – neither of which pursuits involves the rider in *sitting* fully in the saddle for long periods. For that purpose it met every requirement. When it was used for hunting, a purpose for which it was not designed, and one with which Toptani himself was unfamiliar, it was often far less satisfactory. Quite frequently, as a result of the rider's weight being on the saddle for an extended period of time, a 'rock' developed that put the saddle out of balance, causing it to ride upwards and forwards. Additionally, as a result of the imbalance, the very narrow bearing surface of the panel, governed by the narrowing of the tree at the waist, could cause back problems because weight was concentrated over this area instead of being evenly distributed over a wider bearing surface.

Both Toptani and Gibson understood this very well, the latter producing a modified 'all-purpose' pattern that avoided those failings. Manufacturers marketing their own versions of the Toptani were less aware of the problem – in fact, most were

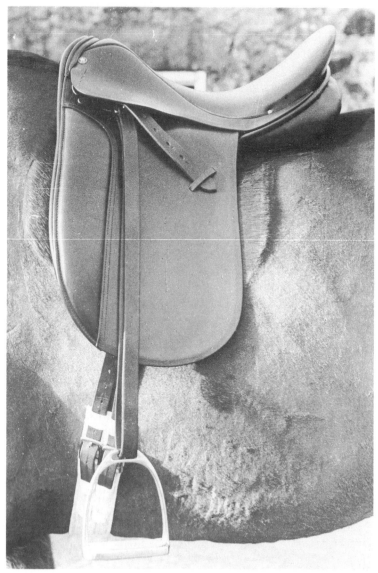

A modern dressage saddle of excellent quality which fails on account of a design fault. The stirrup bar is placed too far forward, if an extended pattern bar had been used the leather would lie in the centre of the flap

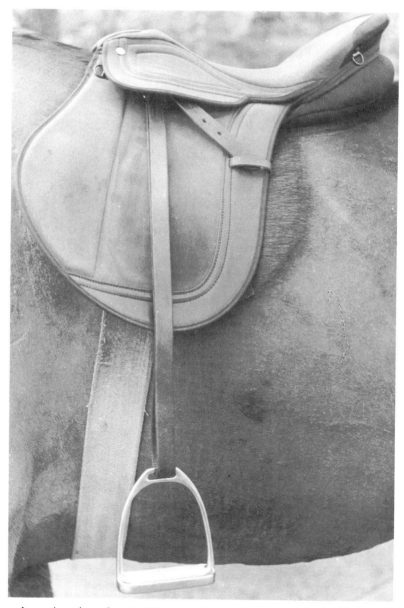

A modern jumping saddle made in synthetic materials which sits well on the back

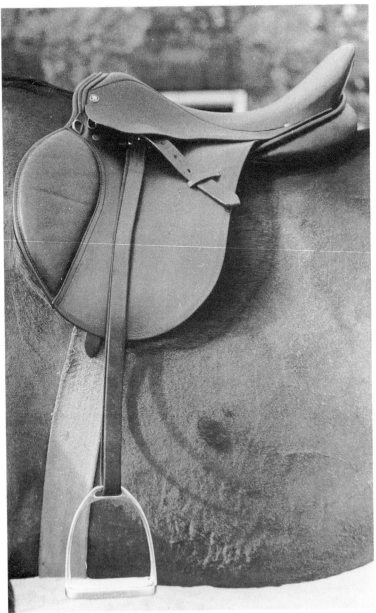

A modern general purpose saddle with a particularly good seat

totally unaware of it. As a result numbers of unsatisfactory saddles came on the market.

The one saddle in which the vertical head was necessary was that used specifically for dressage, a discipline calling for a longer leg position and a panel that was nearly straight cut. The design details of the dressage saddle are discussed in a later chapter; for the moment it is sufficient to understand the proper relationship of bar and head in a saddle of this type. In fact, the principle involved was well established in the military saddles of the nineteenth century, but is very frequently and quite incomprehensibly ignored in modern saddle production. In consequence, we have a reversion to the fault in the old hunting saddle of having the bar too far forward. In a dressage saddle, which, of necessity, must employ a vertical head, the bar has to be positioned further to the rear if the line through the rider's shoulder, hip and heel is to be maintained. As that is impossible using a conventional stirrup bar, a special pattern, an *extended* bar, which allows the leather to be positioned further back under the rider's seat, so that it divides the flap equally, becomes a necessity. A dressage saddle, built on a straight head, or one that is cut-back, which is not fitted with such a bar, is a contradiction to accepted theory and practice and is to all intents useless. (Largely because of economics, but also because they and the public are still insufficiently informed, there are manufacturers in Walsall, as well, let it be said, as in Germany and elsewhere, who make all three basic saddle types, and one or two variants as well, on the basis of a single tree pattern. It works commercially but is otherwise a retrograde practice.)

9: Recipe for Disaster

The very fact that saddles are still made with basic faults in design and construction highlights the extraordinary situation that had come about during the 1970s and was possibly in evidence some years earlier.

As we have seen, neither tree-maker nor saddle manufacturer had any close association with the horse; they knew nothing of physical structure or locomotion, nor were they in touch with equestrian development and theory. Between the wars, so far as the Walsall manufacturers were concerned, this was not a matter of such import as it might seem. They worked to tried and proven patterns and they had the advantage of a network of retail outlets in Britain that were run by working craftsmen who were necessarily in very close touch with the horse-riding public. In their turn, that public, which still enjoyed the experience of the trained ex-instructors of the cavalry schools, was immeasurably more knowledgeable in terms of horse-management than would be possible today.

By the 1970s, however, a far more disturbing situation had developed, one that, to some degree, pertains right up to the present day.

Saddlery was still manufactured by people ignorant of the requirements of the equipment they made and the purposes for which it was intended, but now that failing was compounded twice over. In the first instance, the retail industry had changed. Economic pressures and a new social scene ensured the demise of the old saddler's shop run by a craftsman. Some, of course, survived, and one or two excellent establishments came into being, but by and large the clutter and jumble of the old-time shop was being replaced by smart leather boutiques, often run by trendy young people who might ride horses but knew very little more about their stock than the people who supplied them.

To complete the recipe for disaster, the consumer was no more knowledgeable, and the syllabi for the BHS examinations, although admirable in other respects, were woefully lacking in the emphasis given to saddlery – as, indeed, they are today.

10: The Walsall Twilight

Although the established Walsall companies were turning out some exceptionally good saddles in the 1960s, this was the decade in which the town's staple industry went into decline, abdicating the throne of the world's leather industry and allowing the enterprising German manufacturers to seize the discarded crown. Changes in social and trading patterns were to blame in part, but there is no doubt that the very structure of the Walsall trade and its inability or unwillingness to recognise change were also factors.

The 1974 report on 'The Selected Markets for Saddlery and Harness-Makers Goods', compiled by the International Trade Centre, had this to say about the Walsall situation:

> 'Since the early 1960s, the industry has been plagued by a growing shortage of skilled labour. This is due partly to the traditional *status quo* attitude prevalent among many of the smaller saddlers who have been working in the same way for hundreds of years. They were not prepared for the notable increase in demand in the early 1960s. . . .
>
> 'Finally, the labour shortage has resulted in a high degree of labour turnover within the industry as skilled craftsmen either change their places of employment frequently, being attracted by higher wages or better fringe benefits, or set up their own small saddlery shops in the hope of profiting from the market situation.
>
> 'Overall, the above developments have meant that the traditional English quality standards for hand-made saddlery and harness goods are not always met.'

The criticism was justified and the situation kindly understated. Indeed, 20-odd years later, *Equestrian Trade News*, the journal of the British equestrian industry, was far less restrained in its condemnation. An editorial entitled 'Clean up Walsall' referred to 'the growing reputation of the town for disreputable business practices and inferior merchandise' and it continued in that vein.

The fragmentation of the industry and the activities of the breakaway backstreet saddlers made competition from outside inevitable. It came most particularly from Germany but also from the Argentine, Spain, Switzerland, Romania and, most disastrously for the consumer, from India and Pakistan. (Early imports from the last two countries were so badly made as to be unsafe. They were sold by market dealers, and established retailers would have nothing to do with them. In the end the bad reputation they earned brought the Indian trade to a halt. Today, large quantities of saddlery of all types is still made in Kanpur, India's equivalent of Walsall, for export to Australia and America. In fairness, it is much improved and there is a discernible movement among British distributors to establish ties with the Indian industry, particularly in the tanning and leather-dressing areas where abundant low-cost labour still makes hand-finishing viable.)

The decline of the Walsall trade had its brighter side. Established firms merged to form trading groups and attracted a new type of management, far removed from the old inward-looking conservatism but yet retaining the old craft tradition. Without doubt the best Walsall saddlers still have a feel for leather and an eye for proportion and line rarely found elsewhere. Today, although the town is in some respects still bedevilled by its past, there are companies led by vigorous, imaginative young people that are still able to turn out goods the equal of any made elsewhere in the world, and often better value, too.

Perhaps, too, the degeneration of the Walsall trade was in itself an incentive for the formation of stronger retail organisations, like the British Equestrian Trades Association (BETA) and the retail side of the Society of Master Saddlers.

11: The German Influence

None the less, for the present it is the German influence that remains predominant in saddle production, almost as though Walsall has accepted the philosophy of joining them if you can't beat 'em. (A very good Walsall saddle manufacturer, on a recent business trip to the United States, was complimented by a potential customer on the quality and appearance of his sample saddles: 'They look', said the American, 'just like German saddles!')

The German saddle-makers can take credit for introducing a new look to the saddle, for having pioneered new methods of construction and for adding a new dimension in their attention to the cosmetic appearance of the product, the feature which so impressed Count Toptani.

The best German saddles were, and are, very good. The finish is meticulous and the use of colour and new materials surprisingly imaginative and fashion-conscious. It was the German coloured leathers – browns, blacks, greys, and so on – that ousted the traditional London tan. The German manufacturers, to a man, employed the cut-back head, ignoring the Toptani principle. They got away with it, to a degree, with the general purpose saddle but are less successful when they use the same tree on a jumping saddle. Their dressage saddles are, as might be expected, very good and well in advance of the average Walsall model.

The great strength of the German industry, however, lies not only in its ability to package and present its product but in marketing and promoting it with vigour and consummate skill.

Through the use of soft resilient materials, the German saddles afford instant comfort from the moment the rider gets aboard (which was certainly not the case in the past, when new saddles were often handed out to grooms and 'nagsmen' to be ridden-in). In other respects, however, particularly in their use of a plastic tree, they are no better and sometimes not such good value as the Walsall saddle.

The horse world in general fell for this clever sales pitch to a degree, but Walsall swallowed it bit, rein and buckle without allowing time for the process of digestion. Walsall copied the German patterns, even rejecting the well-proven pigskin seat. Unhappily, the Walsall copyists, particularly the backstreet operators, while embracing the more obvious features of the original, did not always produce articles of equal merit. Out of ignorance, they made some very bad dressage saddles, while some of the others are still lumpy affairs, with rolls and panels far too heavily padded. Fortunately, there are some redeeming exceptions.

12: Materials and Construction

Saddles are built on a foundation of wood or plastic that is called the *tree*.

(Plastic had been used in the manufacture of saddle trees in the 1960s, along with fibre glass. The latter was successfully employed in lightweight racing saddles but was insufficiently stable to be satisfactory otherwise. Initially, plastic trees were also unreliable and did not keep their shape, but these early problems have been overcome and, with certain reservations, more concerned with the shape of the moulds than otherwise, they are as reliable as those made from wood laminations.)

The construction of the wooden tree involves two primary trades, those of the wood- and metal-worker, and two subsidiary ones providing muslin scrim and a glue-based waterproofing.

The dimensions of the tree differ between one pattern and another. It varies also in the shaping of the head, which may be straight, sloped or cut-back, in the fitting of the front-arch and in the overall length. The latter is the measurement taken from the head to the cantle and may range from 38–45·5 cm (15–18 in) in 1·25 cm (½ in) steps. The most usual length is 43 cm (17 in) or 44·5 cm (17½ in), but much depends on the dip of the seat.

The principal division in the wooden tree is between the spring tree and those not having that refinement, which are termed 'rigid'. It is the spring tree that is now in general use. The name derives from the two sections of sprung steel laid along the frame from head to cantle. They give a resilience to the seat that increases the rider's comfort, gives a closer and more direct contact with the horse and allows for the transmission of the drive made through the seat bones. The tree

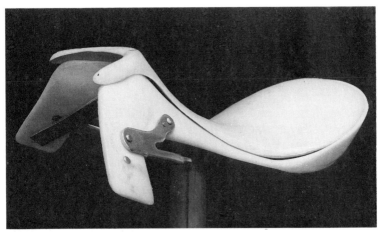

A plastic tree with its shaped foam seat

is also more comfortable for the horse, because of the resilience it gives to the movement of the back.

The modern tree is made from strips of beechwood laminated in moulds with urea-formaldehyde resin. The old-pattern tree was largely shaped by hand from the same wood. It was usually strong enough but heavy, considerably more so than the relatively light modern tree which is of equal strength and has the advantage of being consistent in shape.

The tree is reinforced with metal – either steel or Duralumin which is the lighter of the two. On the underside of the front arch (also called the head or pommel) a gullet plate is fitted; on the top is laid another strip of metal, the head plate, the two being riveted together to form an arched structure of great strength. The cantle is also reinforced with a metal strip on its underside, and the tree is completed by the fitting of the stirrup bars. These are riveted to the tree with two rivets.

The Stirrup Bar

The bars are made from either forged or cast steel, the former being stronger, more reliable and more expensive. Both are stamped according to the method of manufacture. If there is no lettering on the stirrup bar it can be presumed that they are cast and one draws one's own conclusions about the tree's overall quality.

The most common type of bar, which has been almost universally used since the Second World War, although it was manufactured many years before, is usually fitted with a 'thumbpiece' or safety catch. When closed in the 'up' position, the catch keeps the stirrup leather in place on the bar. If, however, the action is sufficiently firm for that purpose, it follows that it will be just as likely to retain the leather in the event of a fall and will, for that reason, increase the possibility of the rider being dragged along with a foot trapped in the iron. Long ago, when the catch was used in the closed position it was regularly oiled to assist the ease of action in both directions.

The majority of catches on today's bars, however, can be moved only with some difficulty, which may be an advantage but is also an argument for the discontinuance of this particular pattern. The weight of consumer opinion is certainly against the continued employment of this bar on the grounds of safety. It is argued that whether the catch is used or not, and every responsible horse organisation urges that it should on no account be employed in the 'up' position, the bar still constitutes a safety hazard. Novice riders, seeing that a catch is fitted, may well presume, and not unreasonably, that the device is there to be used and attempt to close the catch.

Furthermore, the bar adds unnecessarily to the cost of the saddle, as its manufacture is relatively expensive. The more cynical might suggest that this could be why the bar-makers still refuse to recognise the pattern as an anachronism without any practical value.

Quite apart from a recently introduced stirrup bar, discussed later under the heading 'The Shape of Things to Come', there is a simple, practical and cheaper alternative to the safety catch bar,which has been known and made for upwards of a hundred years. This is the bar known as Christie's pattern, a simple hook shape in which the end of the hook is inclined slightly outwards, away from the saddle. It is fitted to that most practical of saddles, the Australian stock pattern, which is used by the most down-to-earth horsemen in the world. It is also fitted to the synthetic saddles that are now becoming a feature of the modern market – but then the synthetics also originated in Australia.

Constructional Faults

Before the saddle is built on the tree, the framework is covered with a muslin scrim to which a glue-based waterproofing agent is applied. This renders it impervious to moisture, whether created by the generation of heat by horse and rider or from any other source.

Although they are not prime examples of precision engineering, saddle trees are generally well built and perform as satisfactorily today as they have done for many years. Even so, and notwithstanding the consistency associated with a moulded product, trees can be made that are out of true and even slightly twisted, a fault that usually occurs in the fitting of the steel springs. There is therefore a need for strict quality control by both tree-maker and saddle manufacturer if the finished product is not to reflect the fault and cause a fitting problem. Quality control at those two points in the production line does not, however, absolve either retailer or consumer of the need to be aware of the possibility of imbalance and to be able to recognise a saddle built out of true.

BSI Tree

The best laminated spring trees are made in Britain, as are some very good plastic ones. There is, for instance, a BSI approved tree that guarantees the quality of the metal reinforcements. It still employs the outdated stirrup bars and the approval is not, of course, concerned with design, but it does, most importantly, specify the fitting by stamping the bars accordingly. It is not, therefore, easily possible for a retailer who has altered the original fitting by the expedient of a vice to pass off a seriously weakened article to the consumer.

Fitting

Three tree fittings are generally recognised: narrow, medium and broad. At least one European tree-maker claims to make trees in a far greater range of widths but 75 per cent of British tree production is concerned with the medium fitting.

Fitting, however, is far from being an exact science. Indeed, it is often concerned with no more than the width of the fore-arch, and in those trees made as one piece in the mould, it is governed by the size of the gullet and head plates. The mould corresponds to the middle fitting, but if a broad tree is required it is obtained by fitting a broader gullet plate and the head is quite resilient enough for this to be a satisfactory solution. Conversely, a tree can be made narrower by fitting a narrow gullet plate. Thereafter, the niceties of the fit can be met by the skilful adjustment of the panel flocking. The same, of course, will apply to trees made of synthetic material. It is not exactly a precise operation, but it seems to work and is commercially viable.

The mould is a very costly item, each one costing possibly a few thousand pounds. A tree-maker providing trees in 1·25-cm (½ in) gradations from, say, 40·5–45·5 cm (16–18 in) will require five moulds for *each* tree pattern; multiply that by the addition of three head fittings to each size and the basic outlay becomes vastly increased.

Not all trees are moulded in a single piece. One British company uses separate moulds for the head, the side-bars and the cantle, the three elements being interchangeable. One advantage claimed for this method of assembly is that the side-bar of the tree cannot become twisted when the head is opened or closed. That is, of course, true enough, although it seems that any displacement that takes place is so minimal as to make no difference to the finished product.

Criticism

In very recent years – perhaps, indeed, within the past two or three years – there has been consumer criticism of the spring tree. Often this has been made by 'experts' whose knowledge of saddle construction, fitting and so on is, alas, not commensurate with their riding ability. Faults certainly exist in some areas and with some particular products but there is no justification at all for an overall condemnation of the spring tree, particularly when it is made on the basis of a false premise. If such criticism is made out of a growing awareness of the saddle's role in equitation, then it is to be welcomed as such, but it will become all the more effective as the riding public and its instructors become more knowledgeable about the equipment that is essential to their enjoyment of the horse.

The use of plastics
Increasingly, plastics are being employed in the manufacture of riding saddle trees and are already commonplace in race-exercise and racing saddles. It is inevitable that the trend towards expansion in the use of modern materials of this nature will continue. The German manufacturers already use such trees almost exclusively and they, like tree-makers elsewhere, are sufficiently sure of their product to provide pretty comprehensive guarantees against failure on any reasonable score.

The trees are of a solid moulded synthetic material, often nylon, that is described as being 'two-way flexible', and, when made up, the seat, like that of the spring tree, has a degree of resilience. The material is impervious to water and has obvious and important labour-saving advantages in terms of its preparation by the saddler. Indeed, it is difficult to pinpoint any positive disadvantage in respect of the material, other than perhaps the possibility of the tree losing its shape with long usage or becoming unduly resilient in one particular area. There is some evidence that the European-made trees may be a little too resilient, so that problems can arise in respect of pressure points.

The synthetics are probably heavier at the moment, and there are certainly design faults in some of the trees currently on the market, but in that respect the same can be said of the conventional product.

Leather

The tree apart, the principal constituent material in saddle manufacture is leather, a living material that has particular qualities. Of course, in 1990 there are saddles made entirely of manmade materials, which is neither surprising nor reprehensible in what is increasingly a synthetic world. These saddles are discussed in more detail later in the text. However, as leather is basic to the construction of saddlery of all sorts, its properties need to be appreciated by horse-owners and riders.

By definition, 'leather is a hide or skin which retains the original fibrous structure and has been treated so as to be imputrescible even after treatment with water' (BSI Glossary of Leather Terms).

Raw, perishable hides are converted into leather by the process of tanning, a word that has its origin in the Amoric word for oak, *tanu*. Oak bark particularly, as well as, to a lesser extent, parts of other trees and shrubs, contain tannin or tannic acid. A solution or liquor made from these vegetable materials is the principal agent in rendering hides and skins imperishable and thus causing them to take on the properties of leather.

In general terms, the process begins with washing the hides in water, then soaking them still further in lime-water. The lime loosens the hair so that it can be scraped off the hide easily. Curiously, the lime has to be used on other skins before it has absorbed sufficient bacteria to become entirely effective for this purpose. The used lime contains bacteria, obtained from the skins on which it has been used previously. It is these bacteria that destroy the hair roots and facilitate their removal.

Once the flesh and hair have been removed, the hides are immersed in liquors of progressively greater strength so that the leather is tanned throughout its substance. (Substance is the word used to describe the thickness of the leather; the greater the substance the greater will be the capacity to absorb the preservative oils etc. used in the currying process.)

Currying begins when the hides are removed from the liquor pits, cleaned in revolving drums of acid, and dried. Currying involves the application of oils, often of fish and marine mammal origin, and tallows (animal fat obtained mostly from sheep). The white film sometimes found on leather is caused by tallow and is nothing more than the 'spewing out' of surplus fat.

Oak bark tanning is still carried out extensively today, but in countries in which the oak tree is not indigenous, other sources of tannin are used. South America uses quebracho wood; in

Australia and South Africa it is wattle bark and in India the bark of the babu tree. These last two produce leathers of a characteristic pink-red coloration; they are sometimes prone to excessive stretching if the tanning is carried out less than thoroughly.

These are all forms of vegetable tannage, which is the method most usually employed for saddlery leathers. For thousands of years, however, people have also used mineral tannages, and many countries still do so.

Alum (aluminium) and salt are used for the famous soft white leathers of Cordova, Spain, while the blue-grey 'chrome' leather, from which field headcollars and sometimes girth straps are made, are the result of a mineral tannage involving chromium salts, after which the leather is dressed with a mixture of soap and oil to make it supple.

Leather for the saddlery trade is made largely from cow- and oxhide. Some pigskin is used, as well as sheepskin (for backings, etc.) and goatskin. There is also a percentage of calfskin and a small quantity of doeskin.

Traditionally, pigskin was used for making the saddle seat and it is still probably the best material for that purpose, although many (almost all) modern saddles, including the German ones, use either panel hide (a supple oxhide 'shaved' to a light substance), less frequently calfskin and doeskin and, increasingly, some specially dressed ox- and cowhide leathers.

By nature, pigskin has little substance, but it is very strong and has great elasticity. When well dampened it can be easily stretched on the prepared saddle tree, and on drying out it produces a neat, tight seat free from wrinkles. Seats made from other materials are probably less hard-wearing; there is a tendency for them to sag in use and, in the case of lighter leathers, these seats can occasionally split.

When the seat is made of pigskin it is usual for the cowhide flaps to be embossed or printed to match the grain of the former. The characteristic bristle markings of pigskin are clearly visible as groups of three. A plain flap is used with seats made from other hides.

In the past, much of the best leather was imported from South America, while the best of all was thought to come from mature Aberdeen Angus cattle. Today, the hides may come from almost anywhere, the advantage of those coming from some parts of Europe and Scandinavia, and the red-coloured buffalo hides from Asia, being that they are free from warble marks and scoring by barbed wire, which weakens and blemishes the hide.

Germany, once more, is in the forefront when it comes to the production of what might be termed 'novelty' hides. The old-established firm of Passier, for instance, has developed a 'secret tanning process' that produces a thick, shrunk leather that is said 'to stretch and expand ... to give a feeling of softness'. At least one leading Walsall firm is making use of this leather, which, while being nothing like pigskin, is claimed to give an 'instant-comfort' seat.

One old-established and highly reputable Walsall firm advertises their use of Schrumpf and Mokko leathers. This sounds like a music-hall duo but it is claimed that Schrumpf on the seat and Mokko on the flaps give greater adhesion and thus increase the rider's security. Schrumpf is described as being 'slightly tacky' and may, as a result, give comfort to those who have yet to acquire a firm seat or whose breeches are made from particularly slippery nylon cloth. (In America, a form of glue is marketed that can be applied to the saddle seat to increase the rider's security!) These departures from the norm have obvious sales promotion potential. One French firm, again of high and worldwide repute, announces its adoption of 'Norwegian Cow' as a medium for its products, almost as though this is the equivalent of making a saddle from the hide of a 'sacred cow'.

None the less (the American glue apart), there are some practical advantages and the industry has to be credited with a genuine desire not only to improve its trade but to do so by offering a better product and a wider choice to its customers.

At least one of the more innovative of the Walsall companies has put its faith and capital in Asian buffalo hide. It uses a stout German doeskin for the seat and a heavy-substance buffalo hide (7 mm thick, no less) for the saddle flaps. The reddish hides, which retain the distinctive skin markings, are naturally thick, but they are also very soft, almost to the point of being flabby. They are said to have a cloth-like texture that allows the leg to mould itself, as it were, to the contour of the horse.

A full hide, however it is dressed, is divided into sections according to the purposes for which it is intended.

The best part of the hide is taken from either side of the animal's spine and it is from these *butts*, sold in pairs, that the very best bridles are made and also the best saddle flaps and skirts. Cheaper saddles make use of shoulder leather, which is stout but much coarser in texture. The thickness or substance of the leather is determined by passing it through a 'shaving' machine after the tanning process.

Colour

Colour in leather is applied by pad staining or by spraying in the final stages of dressing and it demands great skill on the part of the operator if the colour is to be even and the dye fast. There is now some evidence of a return to the old orangey-yellow London colour but the largest call from saddle manufacturers is for a soft, unprinted, well-greased hide in shades of brown or even black and sometimes in greys and greens, too. Many hides are produced with an aniline finish, which is fine, but if the practice persists the manuals of equitation will have to be rewritten, for such leather can no longer be cleaned with spit, sponge and soap – not soap of the glycerine variety anyway.

Prudent saddle-makers affix a swing ticket to their product, warning the purchaser about the possibility of colour loss and advising how the leather should be treated prior to use and thereafter. It is a fact that modern leathers, dressed to the colours that the riding public now regard as being obligatory, do lose their colour and can be easily marked, particularly by rain. Black dyes are the least fast of all and should be cleaned carefully, according to the maker's instructions, before being used. Indeed, the same applies to other leathers, even though loss of colour or marking is not quite so apparent.

Leather, wood and metal represent the essential trinity in the manufacture of saddles but the products of many other trades are also concerned in the finished article. There is merino wool for stuffing panels; felt, wool serge, canvas and pre-stretched jute webs for the seat; tacks, nails and thread, wax and glue and an increasingly large range of plastic materials.

Construction

Despite the introduction of modern machinery and materials and the obvious need to streamline production in the interests of cost-effectiveness, the making of the traditional saddle remains a handcraft in its essentials.

The manufacture of the conventional leather saddle, built on a laminated tree, begins when the tree, with its protective scrim covering, is delivered to the saddle-maker. Before the outer parts of the saddle can be fitted, the saddler has to prepare the tree. The points, the projections of the front arch below the stirrup bars, have to be finished in leather to create a 'flexible' point ending that will allow for minor differences in the shape of the back, slightly increasing the range of fittings available.

The steel springs have then to be covered in light leather to prevent their edges cutting into the panel of the saddle and also to prevent any corrosion that might occur as a result of moisture.

The first step in setting the seat to the prepared tree is to secure taut canvas webs from cantle to pommel. These will have already been stretched, when wet, on a rack. The pre-stretched webs are fixed to the tree with small tacks, called tingles, that are driven through a strip of leather placed over the webs to act as a washer.

Thereafter, the webs, carrying the two rear girth straps, are put over the waist, or twist, of the tree across the seat webs. These, too, are secured by tacks in the same fashion.

The forward girth strap is stitched to a separate web that is either passed right over the tree or is doubled round each bar of the tree.

Once the webs have been covered by a tightly stretched shape of strong canvas, a firm, fairly resilient base has been created on which the seat can be built. Great skill is required if the seat webs are to be fitted with exactly the correct degree of tension.

One web fitted tighter than the other can pull the tree out of its proper alignment, and the subsequent twist will prevent the completed saddle from resting level on the back, thus affecting the balance of rider and horse and risking injury to the latter.

To shape the seat so that it will not drop away at the edges and to save the rider from sitting on the hard edges of the tree, small crescent-shaped pieces of leather, called 'bellies', are tacked to each side on top of the canvas covering the webs.

The traditional and very time-consuming method of building the seat was to overlay the canvas-covered tree with tightly stretched serge cloth stitched down to form the seat shape. A small slit was made in the centre through which the wool padding could be inserted between canvas and serge using a 'seat steel', a thin rod designed for this purpose. The wool was then levelled out with another tool, a twin-pronged 'awl' that could be pushed through the serge.

The cost of such a method today would be almost prohibitive and it is probable that every modern saddle has a seat of latex or some form of resilient plastic.

Finally, the seat leather, whether panel hide, doe or pigskin, is blocked to the seat and fastened in place, the skirts, which lie over the bars, being welted to the latter.

After the girth straps have been stitched to the webs, the flaps, which, like the skirts, will have been cut in a press, can be attached. The edges of both skirts and flaps will have been chamfered, rubbed smooth with glass paper and sealed with a specially prepared stain matching the colour of the leather. An additional and unnecessary finishing touch can be added by stitching all the way round the edge of the flap and the skirt. The practice has nothing to commend it and the additional work involved only adds to the final cost.

The last stage is the fitting of the panel and the underflap (the sweat flaps). After the points have been inserted in the point pockets sewn to the panel, it is secured to the saddle across the fore-arch and round the seat.

Modern production methods employ a staple gun to fasten the panel to the tree. It is efficient and saves the time involved in hand stitching the two together. Panels are largely machine-sewn but some handwork is still required. They must be made with great accuracy if they are to fit straight and true. Stuffed panels have to conform to the shape of the tree. They must be evenly flocked throughout the bearing surface and be sufficiently firm while retaining a degree of resilience.

Panels may vary in type. They can be cut from felt and covered with leather or made from alternate layers of felt and latex. Some saddles employ a moulded foam plastic panel and this practice is likely to increase as new materials come onto the market. (Some years ago a pneumatic panel – an air-cushion – was developed in France but, for various reasons, it did not find acceptance.)

Obviously, there is plenty of room for short cuts in the saddle's construction and also many opportunities to use second-rate materials. The final price will certainly be lower to correspond with the quality of the materials and the level of craftsmanship but the end product is unlikely to be satisfactory to either horse or rider.

13: Synthetics

It seems inevitable, in this synthetic world of advancing technology, that there would one day be a saddle constructed from manmade materials by an innovatory process.

The first riding saddle made from synthetic materials arrived a decade or more ago in Australia. It was preceded by racing and race-exercise saddles and was made by Bates Saddlery, a large Australian saddlery company with worldwide interests. The first samples were made for a racehorse trainer who liked to take his horses into the sea and was tired of spoiling good leather saddles. Bates produced a virtually waterproof saddle of woven nylon material bonded over a multi-structured, closed-cell foam, from which a range of saddles was developed.

Before long another firm of Australian origin joined the synthetic market. This was Thorowgood and, for the moment, Thorowgood and Bates, the latter marketing its product under the brand name Wintec, are the only manufacturers of consequence in this field. Both companies make use of solid moulded nylon trees following the shape of the German patterns. Wintec offers an interchangeable gullet plate in three fitting widths to ensure a near-accurate fitting and the products of both companies seem to fit backs just as well as the conventional German and English models.

Uninhibited by accepted practice, the two companies use modern assembly-line production methods, and both, for the present, use a wool-stuffed panel.

It is necessary to qualify the use of materials and construction methods by the phrase 'for the present', because the synthetic process is subject to almost continuous change. In this lies the great strength of the synthetic saddle manufacturers. They are not afraid to experiment nor to spend money on research. Their

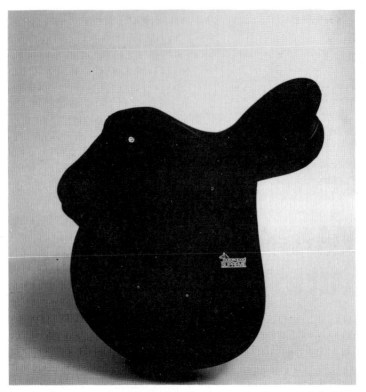

A general purpose saddle made from synthetic material. These saddles are very light, easily maintained and much cheaper than the conventional and longer-lasting leather saddles

open-minded approach, combined with their experience of design engineering, effective production and marketing skills, enables them to design products to the market requirement and to sell them very competitively.

At present, like those of conventional saddle-makers, not all their patterns are perfect but in general they can produce some types, particularly the general-purpose, cross-country saddle, that, in terms of design, are better than some of the English patterns and most of the European ones.

The advantages of the synthetic saddle are these:

1 *Lightweight* – often no more than 2·75 kg (6 lb);
2 *Instant comfort* – or nearly so, for they require a minimum of riding-in;
3 *Easy maintenance and washdown cleaning* – because of the 'button in' production methods, parts are easily replaced at low cost, although there is little to go wrong. Girth straps, for instance, are of nylon and attached by unobtrusive metal links to nylon tree webs. It is difficult to envisage a situation when a girth strap could break. Cleaning is accomplished by washing down with a sponge;
4 *Improved grip* – well, you won't slip about on them, certainly, because of the texture of the material;
5 *Choice of colour* – not very important, perhaps, but it is available and far more discreet than initially when the 'fashion' aspect was accentuated;
6 *Price* – about half that of a run-of-the-mill leather saddle and less than one-third of a top of the market product.

Neither manufacturer claims that their product will last a lifetime and as a substitute for etchings to hang on the walls of your home (in the manner of Count Toptani), they would not be an immediate choice. However, the synthetic materials, already well developed, will improve, as will design, and there is no reason to think that the synthetic saddle will not obtain general acceptance, on its merits, within the next decade.

Of course, there will always be a place for the leather saddle, which has its own sterling qualities and an aesthetic appeal unlikely to be matched by manmade materials, but that position will be occupied by only the very best in terms of materials, construction and design. Otherwise, the second-rate leather saddle, not reaching the highest standards in those respects, will be hard put to compete with a synthetic product in an increasingly synthetic world.

14: Saddle Fitting – the Horse

Although the fitting of modern saddles falls a long way short of the exactitude achieved with military saddles by the professional cavalry officers of the nineteenth century, like Nolan and Dwyer, or by their successors in the British Army between the two world wars, the principles of saddle fitting remain unaltered by the passage of time, even if they are not always sufficiently appreciated.

A properly fitted saddle is one that is constructed so that when the rider is in position it:

1 Conforms to the shape of the individual horse's back;
2 Avoids the possibility of damaging any part of the back with which it comes into contact;
3 Affords complete comfort;
4 Does not restrict the potential for natural movement.

Those are the basic overall requirements and they are interdependent. When it comes to the actual fitting of tree and saddle, further specific principles have to be considered. None, however, is likely to be met fully unless the saddler fitting the saddle, or the owner, has some knowledge of the back structure for which the saddle is intended and appreciates that the choice of a saddle and its fitting will be governed as much by the conformation of the individual as by the purpose for which it is intended.

As far as the saddle is concerned, the relevant structure is the chain of bones making up the spine, the ribs, the scapula (shoulder-blade) and the connected and protective musculature, in particular the trapezius, the triceps and the big latissimus dorsi.

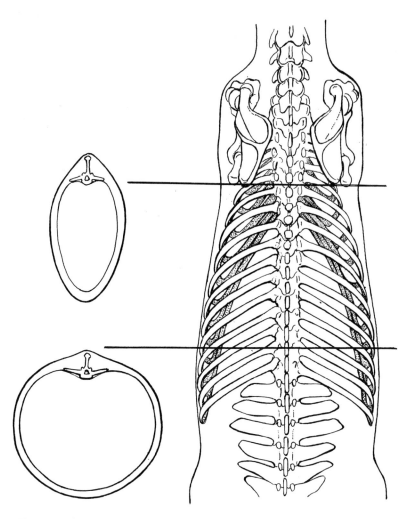

The horse increases progressively in width from the front to the rear and the cross-sections of the vertebrae (*left*) show the difference in shape. For the purpose of saddle-fitting the back extends from behind the scapula to the last rib. Any conformational failing affects the fitting of the saddle adversely

The back is comprised of 18 vertebrae (thoracic or dorsal vertebrae) that are arched and so give strength to a structure that was not actually intended or designed to carry weight. (Indeed, the vertical human spine, a far stronger construction in comparison to the horizontal equine one, is far better suited to the purpose of weight-carrying.) In the horse's back, the first 13 dorsal vertebrae, as Dwyer observed, incline backwards, while numbers 15–18 incline forwards, leaving vertebra number 14 as the keystone of the arch.

The horse has 18 pairs of ribs, the first eight of which are termed *true* (sternal) ribs and are secured to both vertebrae and the sternum bone. The remaining ten ribs are the *false* ribs (asternal) and are attached only to the vertebrae.

The well-made riding horse has long, well-sprung but fairly flat sternal ribs, allowing the rider's thigh and leg to lie easily behind the triceps muscle. These ribs, of course, contribute to the essential depth of girth, which allows room for large lungs and for them to be fully expanded. The asternal ribs are more rounded and shorter, although if they are too short they will present their own problems, in particular causing the horse to 'run up light' (like a greyhound) when put into work. Shortness in the false ribs, combined with a lack of roundness, may also result in the saddle sliding backwards. Usually, in almost every saddle, the tendency is to move the opposite way, i.e. forwards, a failing accentuated by low wither formations and when the development of the triceps and trapezius is insufficient or has been lost by a drop in condition. Wasted dorsal muscles will also contribute to the problem.

The head of each rib is jointed into every link of the spine, an arrangement that permits movement in the ribs for the purpose of respiration. The much stronger true ribs, an essential element in saddle fitting, move very little. Furthermore, in fitting the saddle it has to be remembered that because of their additional attachment to the sternum, the curving of the ribs increases from front to rear. The body is narrowest between the first two true ribs and widest between the last of the false ribs. As a result the shape, when viewed from above, is triangular. Any deficiency in proportion, size, length, symmetry and so on in this middle portion of the horse makes the job of fitting the saddle, so that it stays well in place, that much more difficult.

The upper part of the thoracic vertebrae form the ridge of the backbone and can be felt quite easily. The lower part, which is the spine proper, is heavily covered with flesh and is not, in consequence, so vulnerable to injury as the upper part, which cannot bear weight without becoming inflamed, thus promoting a whole variety of back troubles.

There is very little movement in the thoracic vertebrae but there is some, however slight, and it is of the greatest importance to ensure that this is not affected by the saddle. Injury to a single vertebra reduces movement throughout the whole column to a point where it is hardly significant and this, obviously, is reflected in the outline and action.

The back extends from the last bone of the neck to the last of the ribs. Much of the backbone, however, lies behind the scapula (vertebrae 1–7, in fact) and so, for the purpose of saddle fitting, the back is considered to be the part from the rearmost position taken up by the scapula in movement to the last rib.

The loins lie between the last rib and the quarters and are composed of five bones. Out of them, at right angles, grow long thin processes that are not found in the backbone. There are no ribs here. The length of the processes governs the width of the loin. The greater the width, the stronger it will be and the more effective will be the propulsive force of the quarters.

However strong it may be, the loin cannot carry weight without injury being caused and the movement becoming wholly inhibited. Therefore, the saddle must *never* rest on the loin.

Another absolutely crucial factor, rarely emphasised in instructions on saddle fitting and too often disregarded by saddlers and riders, is the critical relationship between the saddle and the scapula. It is no exaggeration to say that where there is a noticeable restriction in the movement and a corresponding reduction in the performance level, it can as often be traced to the saddle interfering in some way with the freedom of the shoulder blade as to any other source. In certain instances, when, for example, the slope of the scapula is rather less than desirable, the interference caused by the saddle can result in the horse stumbling badly enough to come down.

In the horse, an animal that has no clavicle (collar bone), the forelegs are attached to the trunk by muscles and ligaments, no joints being involved. The trunk is therefore slung within the cradle formed by the legs.

The scapula, a fan-shaped bone, lies flat on the surface of the ribs and moves backwards and forwards in the process of locomotion. Obviously, if the movement of the blade is obstructed by the saddle, either in respect of the fore-arch of the tree or the cut of the panel, the stride will be shortened, the horse will become tired more quickly and the overall efficiency of the movement will be impaired to the point where the horse may be brought down.

All these factors govern the position and the shape of the saddle which, it will be appreciated, has to rest on either side of the backbone, on the ribs, or rather on the big muscle lying over them. So long as this muscle is large, well developed and well nourished, all is well, for it saves the bones and the skin from injury. Without it, the saddle would bear directly on bone, with disastrous results; the blood supply to the skin would also be cut off by undue pressure, the skin would die and a gall would be the result.

The manual *Animal Management 1933*, published by the War Office, having ruefully made the point that had horses been intended to carry a weight or pull a load some special protection would have been supplied for the purpose, contains this pertinent sentence: '. . . the construction of the back is such that it lends itself to injury, and invites trouble by the very peculiarity and delicacy of its organisation'.

The problem would not be so complex were it not that the conformation of the equine back varies so widely. The difficulties are reduced to acceptable levels when the conformation is correct in terms of proportion, symmetry and the strength of the components. It is increased when the opposite pertains. The saddle, however good, cannot compensate for conformational deficiencies and is very likely to make matters even worse. It follows, therefore, that the conformation of the horse is critical to the subsequent fitting of the saddle and that, realistically, it is better to discard an animal exhibiting extreme conformational defects.

Unhappily, too many horse-owners (and saddlers) know too little about conformation and do not sufficiently appreciate its effect upon performance, soundness and, in our context, the fitting of the saddle.

Fitting of the Tree

As a beginning to the correct fitting of the saddle and the first step in the achievement of all other objectives, it is absolutely necessary for the tree to fit the back – if the tree does not fit, neither will the completed saddle.

Too *broad* a tree will press on the wither; too *narrow* a tree will pinch at the end of the points (the extensions below the side-bars) lower down on either side of the wither; too *long* a tree may put pressure on the loin; too *short* a tree will concentrate the weight over too small an area, particularly if the rider is generously proportioned. The guiding rule is that 'the plate must be large enough for the joint' and those broad in the beam should therefore insist upon the seat being wide enough to prevent them from overlapping it.

Too broad a tree cannot be adjusted by stuffing the panel heavily, it will only make matters worse and throw the saddle out of balance. To remove stuffing from a narrow-treed saddle in the hope that it will fit a broader back is equally ineffective and pinching will still occur. On no account should a saddler be allowed to alter the original fit by pulling in the fore-arch or forcing it outwards: the head will be weakened irrevocably. (The stamping of the size on the BSI tree is designed to prevent this malpractice.)

Long points on a tree seriously limit the capacity of the latter to fit all but a narrow range of backs. The argument that the long point prevents the saddle from slipping over is fallacious, for it causes more problems than it will ever prevent. On the whole any excessive length below the stirrup bar is to be avoided.

In a perfect world the tree would be fitted to the back before the saddle was built. In this one, that is impractical and in general it can be taken that if the tree is of an appropriate fit the completed saddle will follow suit, minor adjustments being made by regulating the stuffing of the panel. It is by no means a precise method and it may be that, initially, the saddle will stand somewhat high but after a little use the wool stuffing settles and conforms pretty well to the contours of the back.

A new saddle should, in theory, and in practice also, be regulated after three months or so when the wool has padded down. It is, however, a skilled job which, today, is not always carried out sufficiently well. In any case, it is necessary for the saddler to take a template of the back. This can be done with a pliable piece of metal or plastic which can be shaped to fit the back just behind the wither, then at a point some 20 cm (8 in) further to the rear and finally along the length of the backbone. The resultant shapes can be transferred onto a stiff card and should provide a reasonably accurate guide for the saddler undertaking the panel's regulation.

Fitting of the Completed Saddle

The saddle is put on in advance of the wither and then slid into place in the direction of the lay of the hair. When the rider is in position, the saddle fitting has to observe what amount to specific principles.

1 *There must be* **clearance** *of the spine along its length and across its width.*

This will involve the fore-arch being clear of the wither to the extent that it is possible to insert three fingers between the two. Similarly, there must be no direct pressure at the cantle. To check that the seat at its centre does not come into contact with the backbone it is necessary to stand close behind the horse, possibly using a stool to obtain sufficient height to see easily. It should be possible to see 'light at the end of the tunnel', i.e. at the saddle's head.

The clearance across the width of the vertebrae forming the backbone is obtained by the channel dividing the two sides of the panel being broad enough to allow not just for the upper spinous process but for the much wider base as well, even though the latter be deep-seated and, in the conditioned horse, protected by flesh. In fact, the saddle must rest fair and square upon the ribs and the muscles covering them.

In general, sometimes because of the shaping of the tree at the waist, and more often because of an inaccurately built and fitted panel, the channel is not broad enough. In most instances it needs to be at least 6·25–7·5 cm (2½–3 in) wide and it should maintain that width throughout its length.

In use, it is possible for the channel of a cheap saddle, and occasionally for that of an expensive one also, to close as the two sides of the panel move inwards. Pressure is then put directly on the backbone.

2 *The saddle must not impinge on the free movement of the scapula.*

The effects of obstructing the scapula have already been discussed.

On a well-made horse, with a good, sloping shoulder, the problem should not arise. On horses less well equipped in that department, the saddle does frequently interfere with the action in front. In this respect, the fitting of saddles to Arab horses will also need careful attention. The Arab shoulder is not necessarily or always upright, but it is *different* in its relation to the withers, which are not always clearly defined and, indeed, are often low, as well as in respect of its juncture with the humerus.

Horses with obviously upright shoulders, widely spaced at the top, and with poor wither formation, are particularly at risk from a saddle bearing upon the scapula. In these instances, the slope of the head and the forward inclination of the points may be the cause of interference but often the fault is in the panel and flap being cut so far forward as to lie on the shoulder blade instead of behind the triceps.

This is a notable fault in many of the less well-made modern saddles but in the end the fault must, for the most part, lie not with the saddle but with the conformation of the individual horse. The only way to deal with it is to choose a saddle with a relatively upright head and a panel cut closer to the vertical. Thereafter, one might resolve in the future to buy a better-made horse.

3   *The panel has to bear evenly upon the back in its entirety and over as large an area as possible, so that the rider's weight is distributed over the whole bearing surface.*

If the tree has an exaggerated dip in the seat, the weight will be concentrated over the waist of the saddle. The pressure exerted over so small an area will prevent the circulation of blood and cause, if not visible galling, then deep-seated bruising, which is, if anything, far more serious as it is not apparent in the early stages. The area over which the weight can be distributed is limited by the size and shape of the panel. (Ideally, from the horse's viewpoint, the panel should be made without waisting in two well-padded square pieces and fitted to a 'Renaissance-type' tree, high at the front and back and positioning the rider directly over the fourteenth vertebra, *à la* Dwyer. But that would not do for modern competitive sport, a matter discussed later in this chapter.)

As a corollary to Point 3, the *balance* of the saddle must be considered in longitudinal and lateral terms. If the balance is wrong and the saddle out of true, it will be impossible for the panel 'to bear evenly upon the back' or for 'the rider's weight ... to be ... distributed over the whole bearing surface'. None the less, it is so important a requirement that it is worth examining under a separate heading.

3a   *The panel must be in longitudinal and lateral balance. Furthermore, the tree must be 'true', not twisted.*

If the panel is stuffed more at one end or the other, it is easy to see that the distribution of weight will be affected adversely. Similarly, a panel stuffed more heavily on one side or the other will create a lateral imbalance that will have the same inhibiting effect upon the movement.

A *twisted* tree will also cause the rider's weight to be thrown to one side or the other and will prevent its even distribution over the panel's bearing surface. A twisted tree can be the fault of either the tree- or the saddle-maker, but it is just as likely to be the fault of the rider.

The failing usually occurs in laminated spring trees but it can

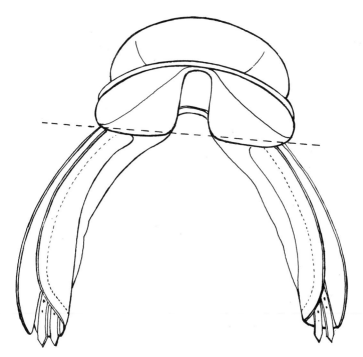

A twisted tree viewed from the rear. It creates an immediate imbalance detracting from the rider's performance; inhibiting the horse's movement; causing unlevelness in the action and is likely to damage the back seriously

also occur in the plastic varieties. The tree (and the spring) can easily be twisted if the rider continually mounts from the ground and, to help the process, grasps the cantle in the right hand. To mount from the ground correctly, the right hand should be placed over or just behind the waist of the seat where the rear of the flap is fastened to the tree. The best advice that can be given is *do not* mount from the ground: get a leg up or use a mounting block. It is easier for the rider and less disturbing for the horse and the position of the saddle on its back.

The rider may also contribute to lateral imbalance by sitting more heavily on one side than the other, often collapsing the hip and sometimes having the leathers adjusted unequally. The answer, for the sake of the horse, the saddle and the rider, is for the latter to take riding lessons.

3b *The panel must be free from irregularities.*

Even the smallest lump or unevenness in its surface will cause a pressure point capable of producing a sore back. Think of walking five miles with a wrinkle in your sock.

4   *While conforming in all other respects, the saddle should fit as close to the back as possible.*

Saddles that are stuffed so heavily as to stand high off the back cause friction because of their ability to shift from side to side, a failing accentuated by the tired rider who shifts his weight from one side to the other. Friction, like pressure, is a source of soreness.

The Effect of Conditioning and Training

The conditioning of the horse has an obvious relevance to saddle fitting. A horse in poor condition is always likely to suffer injury from the saddle, however carefully it is fitted.

Conversely, it is hardly sensible to use a saddle for any length of time on a grossly fat horse. Apart from the difficulty of finding a saddle to fit, fat, soft horses gall very easily. The back needs to be hard before being subjected to anything but short periods of pressure.

(The practice of helping along the hardening process by applying surgical spirit to the back and girth areas – or even salt and water – was a good one and it is a pity that it has gone out of fashion, but then perhaps it may be that many horses are no longer properly conditioned for the work required of them.)

Training is equally relevant. The well-schooled horse will have an equal development of muscle on each side of the spine, which is an obvious advantage for the lateral balance of the saddle. Less well-schooled horses will almost always have more pronounced muscular development on one side, usually, in fact almost always, on the off-side of the body – which, of course, is why the animal turns easily enough to the left but less easily to the right, the last movement being obstructed by a block of ungiving muscle.

Furthermore, the schooled horse will not be on its forehand (i.e. carry excessive weight on the front end rather than engaging its quarters beneath the body). As a result there will be less likelihood of the saddle slipping forward. Additionally, the

The site of common injuries caused by the saddle: 1. Front arch too wide; 2. Front arch too narrow; 3. Seat sinking or tree weakened so as to bear on the back; 4. Saddle bearing against rear of scapula; 5. Sweat flap or girth attachment chafing; 6. Girth galling; 7. Imbalance due to insufficiently flocked panel (concentration of weight)

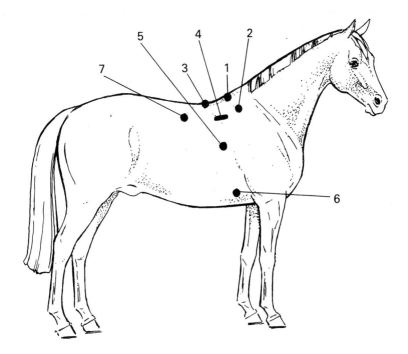

horse will move in an acceptable rounded outline that again contributes to the maintenance of the saddle's position. Hollow-backed horses, the upside-down sort, invite the best of saddles to shift forward, the girth often chafing behind the elbows.

Finally, the schooled horse is a straight horse. That is, the hindfeet follow directly the track of the forefeet, rather than being carried to the outside of the latter. The balance of the saddle and of the rider is therefore unaffected.

It is easy to choose a saddle for a well-made, schooled horse in good condition and to fit it to its back in the knowledge that, all else being equal, no problems will arise. It is very difficult to do the same for the horse of an opposite inclination – there has to be a moral there somewhere.

Results of Bad Fitting

Pain or discomfort in any degree is inhibiting. Ill-fitting saddles, out of balance and not conforming to the principles of good fitting, detract significantly from performance. The movement is restricted, the back stiffens and hollows to compensate and resistances of all sorts are created, often becoming apparent in the mouth. If the saddle pinches or causes discomfort during the act of jumping, refusals are likely to occur, particularly in the less confident or courageous horse. The bold horse, on the other hand, may quickly become a dangerous tearaway, rushing wildly at its fences in order to get the whole unpleasant business over as soon as possible. A stress situation develops, the horse becomes tense and a variety of behavioural problems may arise.

Back Injuries

Not surprisingly, in view of the standard of competitive sport, back injuries are fairly frequent occurrences. Quite often, however, injuries to the back are caused as much by insufficient attention to saddle fitting as by falls over fences – and this is so in the best regulated yards and at the highest levels.

Have the back examined professionally if the horse's action is impaired in any way; if, for instance, the extension is restricted, the hindlegs are insufficiently engaged, the paces become unlevel or there appears to be uneven flexion in the hocks (which might or might not be an incipient spavin), and particularly if there is more than usual evidence of the off-hind being carried sideways away from the track of the forefeet; even, indeed, if otherwise inexplicable resistances develop in the mouth.

But do, also, check the saddle fitting very carefully.

15: Saddle Fitting – the Rider

So far the saddle has been considered almost entirely in relation to the horse, which is proper enough. Indeed, this was the approach taken with the design and fitting of the military saddle. Beyond positioning the rider centrally, where he would be the least possible encumbrance to the horse, and providing points of attachment for his equipment, little consideration was given to his comfort. The McClellan saddle made no concessions in that respect nor, in essence, did the military compilers of the British *Animal Management 1933*. They were immensely concerned with the horse's welfare and with keeping bodies of cavalry effective under prolonged field conditions, but they dismissed the needs of the rider in one curt sentence: 'The seat is a convenience for the rider; a blanket laid over the tree would do as well'.

Today's sporting activities, in whatever field, have reached remarkably high standards and the equipment of the athlete has developed commensurately. The tennis racquet, the javelin, the running shoes and the ski gear of half a century ago, for instance, would find no favour today and would probably limit the level of performance.

Horse sports are not dissimilar, except that the design of the equipment used has to take account of the needs of two beings, the equine and the human, and those of the latter have to be met in much the same measure as those of his partner.

For the rider to be effective, it is very necessary for his equipment to be supportive in every way. A good saddle, designed to meet modern theory and practice, does not necessarily produce a competent rider overnight but, like 'the fine silks' that 'don't make a lady', it helps.

Conversely, a saddle that positions the rider incorrectly and prevents his use of effective aids detracts not only from his performance but from that of the horse as well, for if the rider is not in balance with his horse the latter is also unbalanced and forced to expend extra energy in adjusting its equilibrium.

To be realistic, the modern saddle has to become a compromise between the essential requirements of the horse and the needs of the rider. Increasingly, it becomes a precision instrument and it is sometimes felt that in some areas the scales are tipped rather too much in the rider's favour, but to what degree remains arguable, for the modern saddle has many advantages as far as the horse is concerned. The near-ultimate riding saddle was that designed by Ilias Toptani for the limited purpose of arena jumping. F. E. Gibson, on the other hand, a better horsemaster than Toptani, and with experience of maintaining large numbers of horses under field conditions, came closest to producing the most effective compromise saddle in the last of his Distas Central Position saddles and the first of his post-war All-Purpose models.

Both, however, would have agreed that the object, as far as the rider is concerned, is to build a saddle that provides maximum *comfort, security* and *control* (all interdependent) while providing the greatest degree of assistance in positioning the body in relation to the movement and therefore as near as possible to the *horses's centre of balance.*

Were it not that the horse has a head and neck (virtually a pendulum with an 18-kg (40 lb) weight on the end of it) the centre of balance of the remaining rectangle would be the same as that of a see-saw — at its centre and passing through what has been termed the centre of movement, the fourteenth vertebra.

With the addition of the head and neck, the centre of balance in the horse at rest and standing normally has been established by experiment (principally by the French veterinarians Bourgelat and Duhousset) as being at the intersection of a vertical line dropped from a point a little behind the wither through the centre of the body to the ground, and a horizontal one, drawn similarly through the body to correspond with the line from the point of shoulder to buttock.

The centre of balance is obviously fluid, moving in accordance with the movement of the horse and the gestures made by the head and neck acting as the combined balancing agent for the body mass. At speed and in extended outline, the centre moves forward. In collection, when head and neck are held high with the face in the vertical plane, the base shortened and the croup lowered on account of the full engagement of the hindlegs under the body, the weight is carried further to the rear, over the quarters, and the centre moves back correspondingly. If the horse moves sideways in the lateral movements, the centre of balance must also shift in the same direction, as it must when a sharp turn is made.

If the rider is to be *in balance* with the horse, it follows that he must position his weight as nearly as possible over the latter's centre of balance. It follows, also, that his task will be made easier if his saddle is constructed with this end in view.

The following words written by Gustav Steinbrecht (1808–85) constitute a salutary reminder of the importance of riding in balance. 'Any movement of the body weight either in advance of the point of the horse's immediate balance, or any movement behind that point or to the side of it is reflected momentarily in the carriage and causes an immediate unevenness in the pace.'

Unevenness is one thing, but think how fatiguing it is for the horse galloping over undulating ground if its rider cannot remain in balance with it. Every time the rider is out of balance with the movement the horse will be compelled to adjust its own equilibrium and these constant adjustments are made through the expenditure of much physical effort.

One might also consider that a rider weighing 58 kg (128 lb) and sitting centrally places an additional 37 kg (82 lb) on the horse's forelegs and 21 kg (46 lb) on the hindlegs. If he sits behind the movement and the centre of balance, 46 kg (102 lb) of his weight could be carried by the hindlegs.

The objectives are achieved by:

1   The dip in the seat that makes it difficult to sit other than centrally, *as long as the tree is shaped correctly*;
2   The employment of a resilient spring seat;
3   The recessing of the bars so that bulk under the thigh is removed;
4   The narrowing of the tree at the waist to prevent spreading

the upper thighs and the shaping of the side-bars to place
the rider in close contact with the horse, a feature that will
be accentuated by a relatively slim, close-fitting panel;

5   The provision of strong forward rolls and the positioning of
the bars so as to assist the maintenance of the leg position
and, in conjunction with the seat, to anchor the lower half of
the body securely.

Toptani's saddle, the inspiration for literally dozens of
modern patterns, was ideal for the purpose for which it was
intended i.e. arena jumping. It did not, however, distribute the
weight over a sufficiently large area to be of use over prolonged
periods, largely because of the narrowed waist of tree and panel.
This, indeed, is the Achilles heel in many modern patterns and
the problem is made worse if a panel is stuffed very full, as the
rounding that results reduces the already limited bearing
surface.

Furthermore, if the springs are not sufficiently strong and the
seat webs are fitted so that they become slack, the underside of
the seat, under the rider's weight, comes into contact with the
spine.

There are many modern saddles that avoid these faults
entirely, but there are also some that do not and the customer
has a right to be critical about an intended purchase – as long as
he or she appreciates the details of design and construction. If
the customer does not have that knowledge, he is entitled to
expect expert advice from the saddler offering the saddle for
sale. (A further failing in some patterns is in the shape and
position of the flap. If it is cut and fitted incorrectly, it is
possible for the back of the rider's thigh, particularly if that part
of the anatomy is generous in its proportions, to overlap the rear
edge of the flap, which is neither comfortable nor conducive to
the maintenance of breeches in pristine condition.)

The last principle relative to the saddle is not, one imagines,
acceptable to the great majority and is probably impractical in
most instances. None the less, it remains in essence unassailable
– *to each horse its own saddle.*

There are always people who have a saddle that fits
everything. It doesn't, of course, any more than one pair of

shoes or trousers will fit every man in a randomly selected group of 10 or 20. In reality, it fits some horses acceptably, some not so well and some not at all. The answer, or the beginning of one, may be found in Chapter 18, 'The Shape of Things to Come'.

16: Saddle Types

There are three principal saddle types covering the major disciplines of dressage, eventing and arena jumping. The eventing saddle, which varies from one model to another, can be considered as being in the centre of the spectrum, between the two specialist saddles, and has to be regarded as being closest to the concept of a general-purpose saddle.

In addition, there are a number of variations. The show saddle and the more practical 'working hunter' saddle, now largely supplanting the former, must be seen as being connected, if only tenuously, to the dressage group, while the strongly built polo saddle is at least a cousin of the 'working hunter' type and has largely abandoned its English hunter saddle origins.

Whether the general-purpose saddle led to the jumping saddle exemplified by Toptani's model or whether it was the other way round is debatable, despite the prior appearance of the short-lived Distas and pre-war Saumur patterns.

The more recent, so-called 'close-contact' jumping saddle, on the other hand, bears little resemblance to the Toptani model and a great deal to the race-exercise saddle, the working poor relation of the streamlined racing saddle, the best of which are of Australian manufacture. (Acknowledged as the finest Australian race-saddle was the legendary Bosca, a saddle made of kangaroo hide.)

Finally, racing saddles apart, there is the long-distance saddle, based largely on the Army Universal Pattern, 'fans' and all, or on the Western saddle, or on a mixture of both.

Dressage

Of all the modern saddles the dressage model is the most

specialised and, possibly for that reason, the least satisfactory in general terms. Ideally, an advanced dressage rider should have a saddle tailored for him or her, with all the care bestowed on a Savile Row suit. In practise, dressage saddles are production models made available in one or two seat sizes. The best, so far, as might be expected, are the German patterns. There are some English copies, one or two of which are good, but many more incorporate serious design faults. Indeed, a lot of dressage saddles (European as well as British) are built on the same trees as those employed for general-purpose models and the conventional jumping patterns, which is frankly a nonsense, particularly when the stirrup bars are identical.

The extended bar

To accommodate the longer leg position and straightened thigh, and to accord with the almost vertically cut panel, it is necessary to extend the bar, i.e. use a longer one that places the leather further to the rear and more nearly under the rider's seat. An ordinary bar carries the leg too far forward, in front of the movement, and is in contradiction to the straight panel and the seat. Essentially, however, the tree needs to be designed for the purpose intended.

At least one significant difference occurs between saddles made on plastic trees and those built on the laminated, usually spring, tree. In the latter the side-bars are turned towards the waist to lie flat on the back and to allow, in conjunction with the narrowing at this point, a closer, lower contact than was possible with the older saddle tree.

The plastic tree, used in many German saddles, is a solid one-piece moulding, rising in a half-moon shape across the waist. Possibly it is also a shade broader and, with the twist at the sides, somewhat less pronounced. The effect is to create what used to be termed an 'artificially narrow grip' between the upper thighs, raising the crutch from the back contact as opposed to lowering it. Which of the two trees is the more effective is largely a matter of individual preference.

Otherwise, the general run of dressage saddles employ a fairly heavy gusset in the rear of the panel in order to maintain a level fit and, it is suggested, to increase the bearing surface, a matter that is at best arguable. All have strong forward rolls, dipped seats in varying degrees and, usually, two long girth straps used with a short girth so as to remove the bulk under the leg that might be caused by the girth buckles. (This short girth pattern was first used by Lord Lonsdale, the Yellow Earl, and for many years was referred to as 'the Lonsdale Girth'.)

Apart from the design faults, which are hardly calculated to help, problems arise in all sorts of other areas because relatively novice riders buy and use dressage saddles before they have learnt how to sit in them. They do so in the mistaken idea that it will improve their riding, which it won't, or because an instructor has advised them to do so – which is often a reflection of the latter's lack of understanding. All too often, particularly if the seat is too short and too deep or the gusset too heavily stuffed, the rider is thrown off the seat bones onto the fork in an attempt to produce a position which he or she is not yet capable of assuming. For riders at club level, and even higher, a restrained general-purpose saddle or one of the 'working-hunter' type that has a little more swell to the panel, is probably a good deal more satisfactory.

A dressage saddle must, I believe, place the rider close to the horse, allowing full and easy contact with the inside of the leg as far down its length as possible. An exaggerated dip to the seat is of no help. In fact, the deep dip, combined with the very full gusset at the panel's rear and the straightened front, contributes to the saddle tilting upwards from the rear and slipping forward – a failing accentuated by the back-seat, driving position employed by less expert riders. The addition of the 'fore-girth' (see 'Saddle Accessories') in an effort to keep the saddle in place is one of the more ridiculous developments in the history of riding equipment.

It is better for the tree to be shallower and have a shade more length to it. The bar must be of the extended type or, ideally, one capable of adjustment according to the required position of the leather and the proportions of the rider's leg (see Chapter 18).

My own view is that the panel should be of alternate layers of felt and latex or of moulded plastic, so that it lies flat and close and can be made thinner than the conventional stuffed panel.

Additionally, it should follow the French pattern in shape. This, of course, presumes that the tree fits the back accurately and is of a suitable shape to make the heavy rear gusset unnecessary. Given that to be so, it brings the rider into something approaching 'bare-back' contact but without pressure being brought to bear on the 'no-go areas' of the back. It comes very close indeed to fulfilling Dwyer's dictum about 'bearing the same relation to that part of the back it is intended to occupy as a mould does to the cast that is taken from it'. The firmness of the panel is unimportant as long as the tree itself is resilient enough to 'give' to the movement of the back. (Another alternative might be an adaptation of the versatile Australian stock saddle, or it might be fruitful to study again the basics of the splendid *selle royale* in one or more of its still extant forms – it might prove to be a source of inspiration.)

Show Saddles

The old-time show saddle has now very largely given way to the more practical 'working hunter' type, although it is still to be seen in pony show classes. Today, even dressage saddles are frequently used in show classes as are those general-purpose patterns that are cut closer to the 'working hunter' line than otherwise.

The conventional show saddle, the 'saddle of deception' as it has rightly been called, sought to show off the horse's front to the best advantage, and to create an illusion of the shoulder being better than it was in reality. For this purpose, it was straight-cut; usually fitted with a skeleton Rugby panel of felt and the seat was flat, so as 'not to interrupt the line of the back'. Just to make sure that the front was not hidden, it was fitted with a fourth girth strap, a 'point' strap that was, indeed, fitted from under the point of the tree. This allowed the saddle to be placed further to the rear (an advantage on some pony backs that might otherwise have encouraged the saddle to slip forward) the girth being fastened on the 'point' and the first girth strap.

Properly employed, the girth straps allow for some latitude in the positioning of the saddle and can help to combat the problem of the saddle slipping forward, a fact not perhaps always realised. Usually a saddle is fitted with three straps. Fasten the girth to the first two and the saddle is held a bit to the rear. Use the middle and third strap and the saddle is positioned further forward. Fastening the girth to the first and third straps should ensure a central position.

However, the makers and users of the show saddle were ahead of the dressage folk in one respect at least, for they employed the extended stirrup bar.

The 'working hunter' saddle is really a scaled-down general-purpose saddle and more elegant than most as it avoids the lumpiness that too often characterises the latter, the supportive rolls being discreet but just as effective, and the cosmetic touches, contrasting flap panels and so on, being mercifully absent.

Event/General-purpose Saddle

The general-purpose saddle, now translated into an 'event' saddle, is the middle-of-the-road saddle for most people. You can ride cross-country in it, do some showjumping, school, compete in dressage tests at club level and you can use it for hacking.

It falls down as a general-purpose saddle when the manufacturer (as well as the retailer and the consumer) fails to differentiate sufficiently between it and the jumping saddle, allowing the panel to be cut too far forward and sometimes also giving the tree an exaggerated dip. (The degree of dip in a saddle depends upon: a) the height of the cantle; b) the tension of the seat webs; c) the strength of the springs employed.)

The majority of event/general-purpose saddles have a small 'thigh' roll on the rear of the sweat flap. It does no harm, but it does no good either, as it contributes nothing to the security of the leg position. It would be interesting to hear from manufacturers, retailers and consumers why it is thought necessary. (I suspect that no one would know.) In fact, in a much larger and supportive form, it appears on a variety of saddles from the Middle Ages onwards and is a practical feature on at least one pattern of Australian stock saddle.

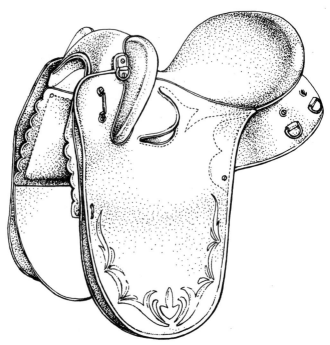

(*Above*) The Australian stock (or buck-jumping) saddle. Strangely there are overtones of the Renaissance patterns. Some stock saddle patterns incorporate a high thigh roll placed on the outside of the flap so as to secure the rider's leg position. (*Opposite, above*) The recessed bar which is a common feature on most modern saddles as well, alas, as the anachronistic thumbpiece or 'safety' clip. (*Opposite, below*) The modern saddle usually has a form of 'thigh' roll – it does no harm but nor does it do any good. The girth straps allow for some latitude in the positioning of the saddle. By employing one and two the saddle is placed a little to the rear; fastening the girth to two and three puts the saddle further forward; using the first and third straps the saddle should assume a central position on a back of good conformation. (The girth 'safes' or guards prevent the girth buckles wearing away the inside of the flap.)

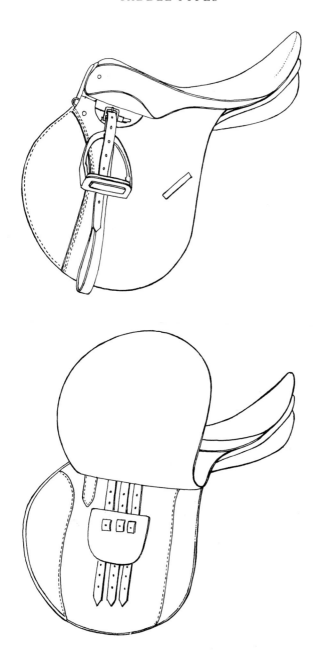

One might imagine it to be a vestigial relic of past glories, rather like the ergot on the horse's fetlock, which was once the pad between the primitive toe formation, but it would be difficult to cast the average saddle-maker in the role of a romantic. No, it is there, according to F. E. Gibson, of whom I enquired many years ago, because in the early Toptanis the forward inclination was such that, after a little use, the two girth straps developed a tendency to ride backwards off the edge of the sweat flap. By placing a roll on the edge of the latter the straps and the girth were kept in place. The problem was pretty soon overcome but the roll remained and that, as it would be put in Rudyard Kipling's *Just So Stories*, was how the saddle got its 'thigh' roll.

Jumping Saddles

In broad principle, the conventional jumping saddle follows the Toptani pattern, varying in detail from one manufacturer to another.

In comparatively recent times, however, the move has been towards the so-called 'close-contact' saddle, inspired it is thought by the saddle developed by the French makers Hermès from the heavy French jumping saddle of previous years that Toptani castigated so thoroughly.

In most of its modern forms, however, it is a derivative of the race-exercise saddle and is built on either the same tree or a very similar one.

Why it should be termed 'close-contact', as though that concept had just been discovered, is something of a mystery. So far as placing the rider closer to the horse is concerned, it certainly does not compare with Toptani's innovative pattern and some of the lumpier copies act in quite the opposite fashion.

The seat, of course, is much flatter and is certainly less supportive of the rider's position. All in all, it is something of a specialist saddle in which very good riders obviously manage very well and it reflects, perhaps, a reaction against the excessively deep seat mistakenly produced by the less expert makers. The average rider with less experience is probably

A lightweight race exercise saddle

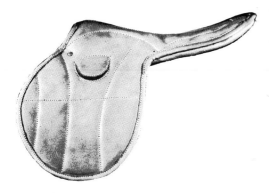

The exercise saddle built on a half-tree, terminating just behind the bars. It provides for an exceptionally 'close contact'

The modern 'close-contact' saddle which is clearly a close relation of the exercise saddle

better off with a saddle of the general-purpose type, while those who are amply upholstered would do well to avoid the less than generous seat provided by the 'close-contact' patterns.

Indeed, to obtain a very close, bare-back contact, the race-exercise saddle, built on a half-tree (i.e. a fore-arch fitted with shortened side-bars extending some 20 cm/8 in to the rear, is far superior in that respect to the more elaborate 'close-contacts').

The race-exercise saddle was the saddle of the training yards and it was always built on a strong tree. It is strange that this essentially utilitarian piece of racing stable equipment should be the basis of so specialist a jumping saddle.

Racing Saddle

Up to the turn of the century, racing saddles, although obviously much lighter, followed the pattern of the hunting saddle, while jockeys rode sitting upright with a long leather

The racing saddle which allows jockeys to ride with a short leather, a practice introduced by James Todhunter Sloan who first rode that way in England in 1897

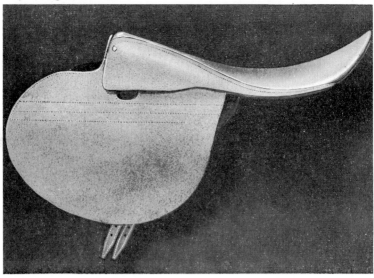

and long reins, as contemporary pictures of the English sporting art school show very clearly.

The crouching style of race-riding, using far shorter leathers and employing a much shorter hold, was introduced by an American jockey, James Todhunter Sloan ('Tod') who first rode in England in 1897. Sloan was also responsible for the style called 'acey-deucey', still employed by American and Australian jockeys. It involved riding with one leather shorter than the other in order to improve the balance and take advantage of the track being left- or right-handed. Sloan left England under a cloud in 1900, having fallen into bad company, and he died in obscurity in 1933, but by then every jockey rode in the style that he had introduced. Therefore, he, too, has to be regarded as one of the equestrian innovators.

To conform to the altered style, saddles were cut with a correspondingly forward flap, although, very surprisingly, certainly in respect of the race-exercise saddle, the American patterns were straighter than the English ones.

Long-distance Saddle

There is not yet a definitive saddle for the sport of long-distance riding but there is, none the less, a noticeable trend towards adaptations based on the military and Western saddles, which is entirely understandable. There is no need for close rider contact in a saddle designed for long-distance riding and any attempt to produce one would be counter-productive. It is, on the other hand, very necessary that the saddle should spread the weight over the largest possible surface and that it should allow the rider to sit comfortably so that he or she is not compelled to ease discomfort by constantly shifting about in the seat. Both the military saddle and the Western one fulfil these criteria, the latter making its concession to rider comfort through the sloped (upwards, towards the head) and often padded seat with its supportive cantle. There used to be a mid-seventeenth-century saddle in the Barnsby collection at Walsall that would make a most effective long-distance saddle. *Plus ça change ...!*

The only danger in employing the military fan tree (the fans are projections of the side-bars behind the cantle) is that in

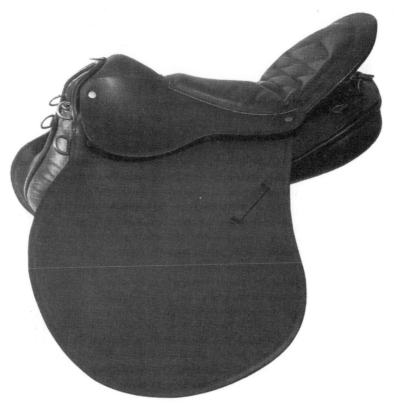

The seat is a bit medieval in style with a strong suggestion of the *selle royale* and the Western saddle. In fact it is a 'Long Distance' saddle

some cases they produce friction over the loins, causing damage to that area. Fans need to be made with an upward sweep but even when this is done, considerable care must be exercised in the fitting.

17: Numnahs

Although it is widely used, the numnah remains a matter of controversy. I have stated that the frequency of back problems in the horse could well be due in part to the design of the saddle and the manner of its fitting, but it would be unwise to suggest that the increasing use of the numnah represents a recognition of that situation by riders. It is more likely to be a case of follow-my-leader fashion and the ready availability in the shops of numerous persuasively promoted and attractively presented products. Make no mistake, however, the modern offering is far superior to the traditional numnahs made of felt and sheepskin. The synthetic materials allow the back to breathe and they are easily kept clean. This was certainly not so with the old-type numnah which could heat the back unacceptably, causing it to become soft and more prone to galling, and which was also impossible to keep clean and in good order without the expenditure of much effort and time.

A viable criticism against the numnah is that it creates a substantial bulk between the rider and his horse, nullifying, to a degree a saddle construction designed specifically to increase the closeness of contact. Some of the modern numnahs are thin enough to be more in the nature of a saddlecloth, preventing the panel from becoming soiled by sweat and grease deposits, and very good they are. The thicker ones, however, like the old types, still add a significant extra bulk under the legs.

On the credit side, a numnah will mitigate the effect of those modern saddles that, because of their construction, concentrate weight over a small area; saddles, for example, that are excessively narrowed at the waist for the particular purpose for which they are employed, or dressage saddles that tip the rider off the seat bones because of the shape of the tree and a too heavily stuffed rear gusset. In these instances the use of a numnah helps to distribute the weight over a larger area, spreading the pressure a *little* more evenly.

A numnah might also help to counteract the saddle that slips forward, a prime failing in numerous dressage patterns. Invariably, the numnah is inclined to slip *backwards*, a tendency that can act to oppose the forward shift of the saddle.

There is, however, a noteworthy new approach in the manufacture of numnahs, which, one imagines, arises once more as a result of the incidence of back injuries affecting movement and outline. There are excellently made numnahs that take no account of the saddle fitting, the matter of contact or whatever. At least one makes use of small wooden balls set into the substance of the numnah, while another employs a stiff, gel-like material. The claims made for these are that back injuries will be alleviated by their use and/or prevented from ever arising. In consequence, action, outline, etc. will be improved.

In a sense they can be viewed as prophylactics, concerned more with the treatment of the symptom than with the disease itself. Their use, none the less, is entirely legitimate in many instances. There are certainly some horses who appreciated the comfort afforded by a numnah and operate better when wearing one – which is the best possible reason for using it. On the other hand, even the very best of these sophisticated numnahs must not be allowed to obscure the prime necessity for saddles to conform to the principles of good fitting, and they must certainly not be employed to keep a horse in work when its condition would best be treated by rest and proper appraisal of the saddle's suitability.

18: The Shape of Things to Come

Synthetics have already signalled the way ahead and all sorts of new developments are likely to be made in respect of panels, trees and coverings.

The most significant advance in very recent times is, without doubt, the introduction of an 'infinitely variable headplate', a precision-engineered piece of equipment that allows the fore-arch of the tree to be adjusted by means of a small tool, inserted into a cog mechanism, to fit anything from a broad-backed cob to a knife-withered polo pony.

The advantages of this headplate, produced for the moment by one firm, Wellep International, are these:

1   The provision of a saddle that will fit, accurately, a variety of back shapes.
2   The ability to alter the fitting of the fore-arch to conform with the changing shape of the horse in work. It will be appreciated that when a horse is brought up preparatory to being put in work for hunting, eventing or whatever, it will carry an amount of soft 'condition' that will necessitate a wider fitting at the front arch than will be necessary after it has been in work for six weeks and has lost much of the surplus fat in the shoulders, withers and back area.

One saddle, in fact, can be altered on a daily basis so as to exercise a number of horses of different conformation or at varying stages of fitness. Furthermore, the owner of such a saddle becomes at once independent of the saddler so far as it would be necessary to regulate the panel to conform to an altered back shape.

These are advantages of obvious consequence, but there are others.

3   The ability to adjust the fore-arch accurately allows for the use of a much slimmer panel of felt/latex, moulded plastic or whatever, as one is no longer reliant on a stuffed or flocked panel being regulated to make good the deficiency of the tree in respect of its fitting to the horse's back.

In consequence, the contact between rider and horse is closer than ever before and, additionally, the bearing surface can be larger. Stuffing a flocked panel in order to raise the saddle from the wither can, in fact, *reduce* the bearing surface, creating a point of pressure, as, if the panel is stuffed hard, a rounded, half-moon shape ensues that presents what is actually a smaller bearing surface with only the top third of the half-moon shape being in contact with the back.

The adjustable Wellep headplate. The cog, altered by the simple key, is capable of infinite adjustment within the overall parameters. It is possible to adjust the head to fit a round-backed cob or a knife-withered polo pony

Wellep's adjustable stirrup bar allows the rider to be positioned precisely, taking into account the length of leg and the purpose required

4   Resilience, an essential quality in the saddle, is provided through the tree, either via the springs or because the quality is inherent in a plastic moulding.

What is more, it is possible to adjust the saddle up or down in order to correct the rider's position, and that leads on to the *adjustable bar*, perfected by the same company.

Fitted to either a dressage or general-purpose saddle (it is unnecessary on a jumping saddle) this allows the trainer to position the rider with great precision. The bar can be taken back or forward according to the purpose required (i.e. forward for jumping in a general-purpose saddle, and moved a slot to the rear for flat schooling employing a longer leather), but the facility extends beyond that. It allows the trainer, by adjusting the bar position, to place the rider in the desirable balance attained by the vertical line involved in the shoulder to hip to heel position, whatever the conformation of the pupil in respect of leg-length etc.

This bar also goes a long way to satisfying the safety lobby, which is rightly enough concerned with riders being dragged because the leather cannot slip off the bar in the event of a fall. The adjustable bar, without a safety catch, is inclined just a little outwards so that the leather can be released easily in an emergency. (That, at least, is the consensus of opinion as there has been no volunteer prepared to test the claim.)

The next step might be a tree made from graphite, like a tennis racquet, with a further adjustment at the rear of the tree that would control the degree of dip, and would also govern the angle of the side-bars. Then there would be a saddle that would conform exactly to the horse's back and would also meet the needs of the rider in respect of position, and so on. Before that, however, the basic tree has to be improved in all sorts of respects, particularly in the formation of the front arch, the alignment of the bars, the seat, etc.

As far as the panel is concerned, the ideal is to produce a panel that is slim but is sufficiently resilient to mould itself to the back while giving all the advantages of the specialised numnah without the latter's bulk.

19: Saddle Accessories

The accessories, or saddle 'mountings', comprise girth, leathers and irons, as well, by stretching a point, as a breast-girth and the too-often-unregarded girth safes.

Girths

Without doubt, the most popular of the present-day girths are those made of nylon or cotton which are, more often than not, fitted with a centre of resilient foam. They are comfortable, effective, easily cleaned and not too expensive to buy. In the same category is the tubular web girth, exemplified for me by the *Lampwick* girth that is both soft and hardwearing. It is the ideal girth to use on fat horses brought up from grass.

The soft web girths have largely superseded those made of *nylon* and *string cord*, although the latter are still obtainable. String cord was probably the better of the two and some very good ones were, and are, made in Germany. Nylon girths, particularly some made in England, with poor quality buckles, are cheap but not nearly so satisfactory. The advantage of string/nylon girths is that the separated strands give a very good grip on the coat and skin which keeps the girth in place. An excellent pattern is the broad girth of thick mohair strands that is made in America.

Leather girths are, of course, right at the top end of the market. The initial cost is high but they last almost forever and they have particular advantages. The grease content of the leather, for instance, when in contact with the warmth of the body, causes the leather to soften very quickly. When a leather girth galls the horse, it is usually because it has rubbed up against the elbow as a result of a conformational fault. A hollow-

3166   FOLDED LEATHER & LAYON GIRTH, 2½in. wide   9/6 each.

3167   FOLDED LEATHER GIRTH ..   2¾in. wide, **10/-** ; Better Quality **12/-** each.

Two types of leather 'humane', self-centring girth fittings. (*Above*) From an illustration in a pre-Second World War catalogue. (*Right*) The Balding patent girth; another illustration from an early catalogue as the price reveals! (30 shillings = £1.50)

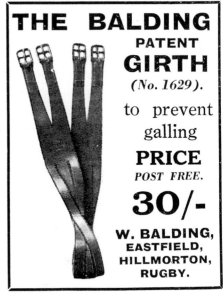

THE BALDING
PATENT
GIRTH
(No. 1629).

to prevent galling

PRICE
POST FREE.

30/-

**W. BALDING,
EASTFIELD,
HILLMORTON,
RUGBY.**

backed horse, for instance, will always cause the saddle and the girth to move forward.

A number of patterns, like the *Balding* and the *Atherstone*, are shaped at the elbow so as to prevent the risk of galling.

A very effective leather girth, not seen so frequently today, possibly on account of its high cost, is the *three-fold* girth made from soft baghide and folded as the name suggests. It was customary for the girth to be lined inside the fold with a strip of saddle or collar serge. This cloth was kept well greased and the

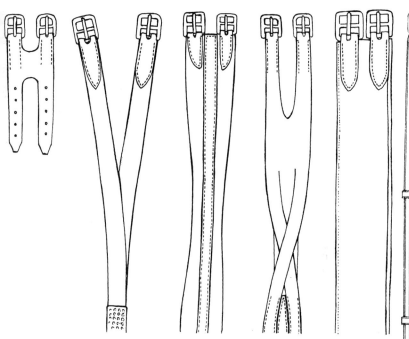

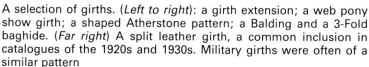

A selection of girths. (*Left to right*): a girth extension; a web pony show girth; a shaped Atherstone pattern; a Balding and a 3-Fold baghide. (*Far right*) A split leather girth, a common inclusion in catalogues of the 1920s and 1930s. Military girths were often of a similar pattern

warmth of the horse melted the grease and kept the leather wonderfully soft and supple. This girth is fitted with the rounded edge to the front, so as to prevent any possibility of rubbing.

Were I to need a new girth today I would try very hard to have one made from a plain strip of stout red buffalo hide, split to form laces, as it were, like one of the old military patterns.

Furthermore, I would then have it made with a humane girth fitting that allows the girth buckles to be set in a V-shape.

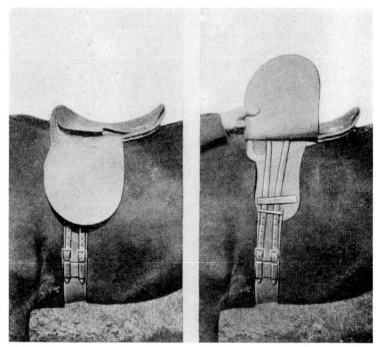

An early version of the short dressage girth in use today was Lord Lonsdale's pattern, popularised by that legendary figure in the latter part of the nineteenth century

The advantage of this fitting, frequently used with polo saddles, is that it centres the girth most effectively, holds it and the saddle very firmly in position and is considerably more comfortable for the horse. Nor, using this fitting, is it necessary to girth up so tightly.

For *show ponies*, there is an excellent girth, made on much the same self-centring principle, which goes some way towards keeping the saddle firmly in position even when the wearer has acquired a certain rotundity. Made from two narrow strips of tubular web, its centre, lying in what in ponies passes for the sternum curve, is covered in 'pimple' rubber, like that used on rubber-hand-part reins or table-tennis bats. By its very nature, it grips the body and the coat like a limpet.

The best and most reliable *web* girths are made of wool rather than cotton web. They are sold in pairs, each girth terminating in a single buckle, and are really the prerogative of the racing man. However, they are also used for cross-country riding, usually in conjunction with a surcingle, the same as that used for racing, which passes over the waist of the saddle and is fastened under the belly. The web is frequently made up in two or even three colours, which gives it a distinctive appearance, and many web girths and surcingles are made with *elastic* inserts to allow for the lungs' expansion at moments of peak effort. Elastic inserts are also incorporated in leather and tubular web girths. Obviously, if the girths have an elastic facility, so must the surcingle, when that item of extra insurance is used. Ideally, if the saddle is to be kept in balance, it is better to have inserts of elastic at both ends of the girth. With a pair of web girths, of course, it is possible for an elastic end to be on each side of the saddle.

Occasionally one may come across a girth and surcingle set made entirely from strong elastic web.

Dressage girths, for use with extended girth straps, may be made from leather or tubular web. I find the dressage *fore girth* an incomprehensible piece of equipment. I understand that it is fitted in front of the saddle to prevent the latter from slipping forward. It may do that, but in doing so there is a risk of galling at the elbow, which will hardly be conducive to freedom of action, and, which is even more inhibiting, it also restricts the movement of the scapula quite seriously. If the saddle slips forward, for Heaven's sake correct the saddle! It seems singularly unintelligent to attempt the elimination of one fault by the introduction of another.

Buckles represent the weakest link in the girth. Very, very few girths break (though elastic sections may perish in time), but buckles, particularly those made of nickel, fracture with frightening ease. The quality of a well-made buckle, preferably of stainless steel, can be judged by the firmness of the tongue, the end of which should lie neatly in the recess provided on the upper bar. Such buckles make the adjustment of the girth a simple enough matter, whereas a loose tongue makes the operation difficult and frustrating. Loose tongues accompany cheap buckles, while buckles fitted with tin rollers round the top bar (calculated to cut into the leather with which they come into contact) are anathema.

To prevent the girth buckles, even good ones, from wearing holes in the underside of the flap it is prudent to fit the girth straps with *girth safes*, a thin piece of leather, slotted on the straps, that lies over the buckles. Thick girth safes make adjustment difficult and add bulk under the leg.

Finally, against the occasion when a fat horse defies all attempts to fasten its usual girth, a girth *extension* will prove to be a good investment.

Breast girths are employed to prevent the saddle sliding *backwards* and may be necessary in very hilly countries or with a flat, slab-sided horse. For racing, when the strains imposed on a lightweight saddle are severe, use is made of the Aintree pattern which can be made, sensibly, of elastic. It needs to be fitted carefully, however, to ensure that it does not ride up and interfere with the windpipe. The 'hunting' breastplates, fastening to a neckstrap, need to be backed with a piece of soft leather or a circle of sheepskin at the juncture of the body strap, passing between the forelegs, and the neckstrap so as to prevent rubbing.

Girth fitting demands some attention from both the equine and the human viewpoint. The choice of girth used, for example, is a consideration. When horses gall easily, a girth sleeve of sheepskin, or a piece cut from a rubber inner tube, may be helpful. If, however, the problem is concerned with the girth chafing the elbow because the horse has little or no sternum curve, the latter can be encouraged by working the horse on the lunge and under saddle with a sleeve of oilskin or plastic wrapped round the girth. It is an effective way of sweating the fat off this critical area. The wearing of a roller in the stable, similarly equipped and carefully fitted, is also helpful, acting rather like a corset to induce the desirable shape. (Do, however, ensure that rollers, and rugs for that matter, conform to the same principles of fitting as the saddle.)

The length of the girth can contribute to the rider's comfort if selected carefully. The ideal is to have the buckles behind the crook of the knee so that there is no bulk under the thigh.

Stirrup Leathers

Leathers, fitted for safety and convenience with the best possible stainless steel buckles, are made from oxhide butts tanned by the oak-bark process, from buffalo hide and very occasionally from rawhide. (Rawhide can be recognised by the characteristic untanned central layer, rather like the filling in a sandwich, that is usually yellow in colour.) In the 1990s, inevitably, there are 'leathers' made entirely fron synthetics like nylon, or reinforced with nylon.

Leathers for children will usually be made in ⅝ in, ¾ in and ⅞ in widths. Leathers for adults range between ⅞ in and 1¼ in. My own preference is for a 1-in leather. The strength of a leather of this width is more than ample if the best quality is chosen and is more manageable than the wider types that will be fitted with heavier buckles.

Ox- or cowhide leathers and rawhides are made with the 'flesh' side facing outwards so that the tougher, more hard-wearing 'grain' side (the outside of the hide that has received the dressing) takes the friction from the eye or slot in the stirrup iron through which the leather passes. The reverse is true of red buffalo hide which is so strong that there is little difference between the wearing properties of either side.

In time, wear will occur where the leather passes through the eye of the iron. This is not of much consequence with buffalo hide but with other leathers it is prudent to shorten the leather at the buckle end to allow an unworn portion to come into contact with the metal.

All leathers stretch in use, rawhide more than cowhide and buffalo hide more still. New leathers should be alternated from side to side to prevent uneven stretching which, of course, would upset the rider's balance. In a perfect world we should ride with an exactly even weight in each iron. In practise, most riders tend to be a little harder on one than the other and that applies even to the best of us.

It is never advisable to use a brand new pair of leathers for a day's hunting, a cross-country or other jumping event or a point-to-point and this applies very particularly to buffalo hide. One might very well find oneself riding uncomfortably long at an inconvenient point in the proceedings.

Once the leathers have lost any propensity to stretch further, they can be trained to lie correctly on the saddle. This is accomplished by taking the nearside iron and twisting it in a clockwise direction before exerting a strong, downwards pull. The iron will then hang naturally at right angles to the saddle and the difficulty of fumbling for an iron with one's toe is overcome. The off-side leather is dealt with in the same way, but here the twist is anti-clockwise.

The loose end has also to be trained to lie pointing to the rear. If a little time is spent pulling the leather into the proper place it will soon fall naturally into position. The practice of tucking the loose end under the existing two thicknesses of leather in order to increase the bulge under one's thigh by 25 per cent can hardly be regarded as intelligent.

A pair of top quality leathers will have the edges smoothly bevelled and the holes punched evenly and numbered. Bevelling the edges is certainly a nice refinement but it also has a practical purpose. The bevelled edge makes adjustment of the leather that much easier as it slides better through the buckle and slips with equal ease on and off the stirrup bar.

Numbered holes are obviously helpful. Mine are punched closer together than is usual ('half-holes') to allow for a finer adjustment of the length.

For those with large horses and short legs, or who for other reasons find it difficult to mount from the ground when that becomes necessary, an extending or *hook-up* leather will be appreciated. The nearside leather is fitted with a hook and slot attachment joined by a short piece of web. When open, this allows the leather to be lengthened by about 15–20 cm (6–8 in) and when the rider is mounted it is a simple matter to slip the slot back over its hook so that the leather is again at its normal length.

(I have six pairs of leathers in my tack room. Four pairs are of the very best oak-bark tanned oxhide in 1-in width. Two pairs have been in constant use certainly for 30 years, the other two, less well worn, are 25 years old. The remaining pairs are 1-in wide red buffalo hide. One pair dates from before the Second World War, the other is 40 years old exactly. All are fitted with stainless steel buckles.)

Stirrup Irons

My own irons are made of stainless steel; each weighs 680 g (1½ lb) and measures 12·5 cm (5 in) across the inside of the tread. I can think of nothing better in terms of utility and safety.

To use irons made of any other metal, particularly that wolf in sheep's clothing called solid nickel, is to invite trouble. Nickel, as well as being an unpleasant yellow colour, will bend and break very easily. A blow against a gate-post is sufficient to fracture an iron made of this material.

The ideal size is one fitting larger than one's boot, but not so large that the whole foot could slide through. The heavier the iron the better, for it will drop away from the foot should one have the misfortune to be dislodged.

The most common of the *safety* irons is the Peacock, a three-sided iron, if we include the tread, the remaining side being made up of a strong rubber ring stretched between a hook and a stud at the iron's base. In the event of a fall the rubber ring becomes detached and the foot will be freed – as long, that is, as the open side of the iron is on the outside of the foot. It often isn't! (Additionally, there is the disadvantage of the tread becoming bent from continual mounting from the ground. When that happens it becomes impossible to maintain a proper leg position.)

There are one or two patterns of *hinged spring irons* that will open to release the foot in an emergency (and sometimes when there isn't one); but the most effective is the straightforward Australian Simplex with its pronounced forward loop on the outside.

Other than the basic pattern there are two, perhaps three, variations. These are the *bent top* irons, the *Kournakoff* and what I would call the *turned-eye iron*.

In the former the top is bent away from the rider's instep and thus prevents the iron wearing away the boot should the

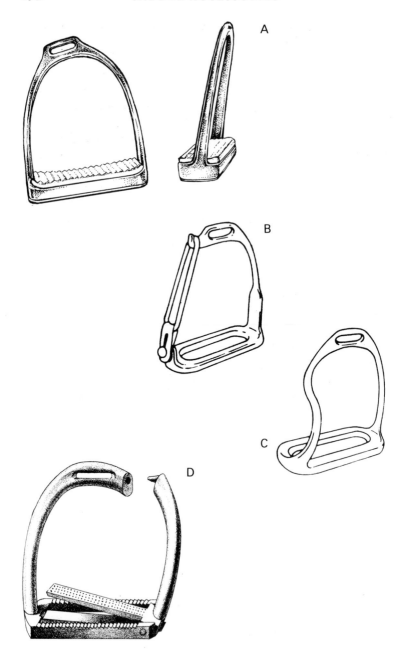

horseman ride with the foot fully home. It will also encourage a lowering of the heel.

The Kournakoff was invented by a White Russian officer, Captain Sergei Kournakoff, who settled in America after the Revolution and was co-author, with his countryman, Captain Vladimir Littauer, of a number of books explaining the Caprilli system. The iron is distinguished by having the eye set to the inside, while the sides of the iron slope forward with the tread sloping upwards. The result is for the foot position to be fixed with the toe carried up and the heel down, the sole of the foot being higher on the outside than the inside. The knee and thigh are therefore pressed inwards against the saddle. It follows, of course, that the irons must be clearly marked 'left' and 'right'. This iron may well be helpful for jumping but clearly it is not suitable for dressage riding.

The 'turned-eye' iron has the eye set in line with the stirrup leather so that the iron hangs at right angles to the horse at all times. North African stirrups have been made to this same pattern for well over a thousand years.

The use of a *stirrup tread* is now almost universal. It helps to keep the foot in the iron and is a comfort to the toes in very cold weather. (The original treads were called Agrippin and were introduced by Mrs Dorothy Popoff, a lady with strong circus connections who settled in England and who was a very proficient High School rider.)

(*Opposite page*)
A = The Kournakoff iron with the eye offset and the tread sloped. B = The popular Peacock safety iron, but one which has disadvantages. C = The 'most effective' safety iron is the Australian Simplex pattern. D = Hinged spring irons of a pattern illustrated in nineteenth-century catalogues

20: Cleaning and Maintenance

Modern cleaning and leather care materials are uniformly excellent and also time-saving, but the old principles remain the same.

Leather has two sides, a 'flesh' side and a 'grain' side. The latter is sealed and waterproofed during the dressing process, but the pores of this living material are, conversely, still open on the flesh side.

The life-blood of leather is its fat or grease content. Some of that constituent is lost every day and has therefore to be replaced.

The loss occurs on account of the warmth of the horse's body. Much more will be lost if leather is subjected to either heat or excessive wetness. Heat dries out the fat content, leaving leather hard and brittle. Water, particularly if it is hot, melts and removes the grease, with the same result.

After riding, remove mud and sweat deposits that clog the leather pores, using a damp sponge. Saddle-soap the leathers and girths using an almost dry sponge and, once a week, apply one or other of the care products to the 'flesh' side where the pores are open.

Sponge dirt etc. off the saddle each day. 'Jockeys', those little black blobs of obstinate grease that collect on the panel and sweat flap, can be removed with a ball of horsehair made up from the tail pullings. Apply a soap or dressing and, at least once a week, give the saddle a proper clean, applying 'food' to the 'flesh' side of the leather, not forgetting the critical girth straps.

Be careful not to apply too much of a greasy substance to the outside of the saddle, lest it come off on your new breeches. Any dressing should be rubbed well in with a light circular motion.

The best thing with which to finish a saddle is a very slightly dampened chamois leather.

Storing Saddles

Keep your saddles on a saddle rack or a saddle-horse. If it is necessary to put a saddle on the ground, place it head-down with the seat towards a wall (if one is available), the cantle resting against the latter. When it is necessary to put it on the ground in a show ring, for instance, lay it down gently, panel upwards.

If you are without either rack or saddle-horse, a thick, soft rope stretched across the tack room like a clothesline is an acceptable substitute.

Do not store saddles in polythene bags, which become subject to condensation. Use a bag or cover of cotton or linen and clean the saddle lightly before putting it away.